STORYBOARDING

STORYBOARDING
Turning Script to Motion

Stephanie Torta
Vladimir Minuty

MERCURY LEARNING AND INFORMATION
Dulles, Virginia
Boston, Massachusetts

Publisher: David Pallai

MERCURY LEARNING AND INFORMATION
22841 Quicksilver Drive
Dulles, VA 20166
info@merclearning.com
www.merclearning.com
1-800-758-3756

This book is printed on acid-free paper.

S. Torta and V. Minuty. *STORYBOARDING: Turning Script to Motion.*
ISBN: 978-1-9364200-0-1

Library of Congress Control Number: 2011923280

111213321

Our titles are available for adoption, license, or bulk purchase by institutions, corporations, etc. For additional information, please contact the Customer Service Dept. at 1-800-758-3756 (toll free).

ACKNOWLEDGMENTS

Stephanie Torta

Many people helped with the making of *Storyboarding: Turning Script to Motion.* Although there are too many to name, I would like to mention a few whose support went above and beyond. First, "Thank you," to Vladimir Minuty for being a wonderful coauthor and an amazing artist and filmmaker, and to all the cast and crew of *Overtime* for their incredible work. Also, Eric, David, Kathy, Geno, and Nancy for teaching me all about the publishing world. To Lisa, Paul, and Kristen and all my friends who gave us their support. Thanks, also, to my brother Jon for taking the time to help however he could, and to the rest of my family. Most of all I would like to give thanks to my Mom; without her support this book would not have been possible. Thank you.

Vladimir Minuty

The making of this book was a rewarding process. Given the many components included in this book—the text, the scripts, film, and DVD—many people had a part in helping to complete this project. I'd like to thank everyone who helped to make *Storyboarding: Turning Script to Motion* a reality. Specifically, I'd like to thank Stephanie Torta for asking me to join her in this project; I'm very grateful for the opportunity. I'd like to thank the cast and crew of *Overtime* for helping us to realize a fun short film. Thanks to my friends and family for your support throughout the making of this book. And last, but never least, thank you to my wife, Angela.

CONTENTS

Acknowledgments   v

Introduction   xi

Part 1: The Storyboard

Chapter 1 - A Brief Background on Storyboards   3

1.1 - What are storyboards?   4

1.2 - Is there only one type of storyboard?   8

1.3 - Why use storyboards? What makes them important?   10

1.4 - What is portrayed in a storyboard?   14

1.5 - Are storyboards different for animated movies
or computer games?   20

1.6 - How are storyboards evolving for the future?   23

Summary   25

Review Questions   25

Discussion / Essay Questions   25

Applying What You've Learned   26

Chapter 2 - Producing the Storyboards   29

2.1 - Where to start a storyboard project?   30

2.2 - Who should be involved?   34

2.3 - What information needs to be gathered?   36

2.4 - Understanding the shot list   44

2.5 - Common types of camera shots   48

2.6 - Descriptions and examples of common camera shots   50

2.7 - How detailed do the storyboard drawings have to be?   76

2.8 - Who benefits from storyboards and why?   77

Summary   80

Review Questions   80

Discussion / Essay Questions   81

Applying What You've Learned   81

Part 2: The Project *Overtime*

Chapter 3 – Preproduction   **85**

3.1 - Information gathering   86

    The *Overtime* script without notation   88

    The *Overtime* shot list unmarked   98

    Location diagrams. Talent and location photographs   102

    Prop and wardrobe list for the project *Overtime*   105

    A director meeting with the storyboard artist
during preproduction   106

3.2 - Refining the information   110

    The *Overtime* script with director notation   111

    The script to rough storyboard comparison   118

    The shot list to storyboard comparison   176

    Location and talent photographs to storyboard comparison   182

    Prop and wardrobe photographs to storyboard comparison   184

Summary   186

Review Questions   186

Discussion / Essay Questions   187

Applying What You've Learned   187

Chapter 4 – Production   **189**

4.1 - Day of the shoot for short film, *Overtime*   190

4.2 - Storyboard-to-actual shot comparison   191

4.3 - Updated boards because of on-set changes   248

4.4 - The shot list-to-film comparison   252

4.5 - Cast and crew credits for *Overtime*   258

Summary   259

Review Questions   259

Discussion / Essay Questions   260

Applying What You've Learned   260

Chapter 5 – Technology and Storyboards   263

5.1 – Conceptualizing for visual effects (VFX)   264

5.2 – Storyboard use in animatics   268

5.3 - Digital creation with touch tablets and screens   270

5.4 - Computer software for storyboard rendering   276

Summary   279

Review Questions   279

Discussion / Essay Questions   280

Applying What You've Learned   280

Appendices   281

A – Glossary   281

B – Miscellaneous   293

    DVD information   294

    Blank storyboard frames   295

    Storyboard practice frames   297

    Extra scripts   298

    Additional Exercises   302

    Cast and crew biographies   304

    References   306

    Credits   306

Index   307

INTRODUCTION

What this book entails

Storyboards: Turning Script to Motion is a detailed look at the filmmaking process as it relates to storyboarding. We follow one short film, *Overtime*, from script to screen and provide an intimate, in-depth look at the key elements involved. Included are the original script, storyboard drafts, director's notes, final boards, filmmaker's commentaries, and the final film. This book provides a play-by-play scenario and closely approximates the actual experience of the process, first hand.

What this book is trying to achieve

Storyboards: Turning Script to Motion is intended to give aspiring filmmakers a realistic look at the storyboarding process. Many books have been written about the creative and historical aspects of storyboarding, this book gives the filmmaker a true understanding of what it is actually like to work on a project.

Storyboards are an important stepping stone to understand the process of translating written word into moving image. This is an integral part of the creative process in the entertainment and gaming industries. It is important for every filmmaker to have some basic knowledge of the process, in order to be better prepared for what it is truly like to work in the field. In this book, we will follow the short film, *Overtime,* from beginning to end to illustrate the experience of all the steps involved in being on a project.

How this book is organized

Storyboards: Turning Script to Motion focuses on one of the many types of storyboards and uses *Overtime* as the example.

The first part of this book is a brief background on the development of storyboards in both the film and gaming industries and why they are an important aid to streamline communication. Common questions are answered and an understanding of the use and preparation of storyboards is given. For a more in-depth history of storyboards and the other industries that use them, we have provided a list of recommendations at the back of this book.

The second part of this book depicts the journey of the film project through completion as it relates to the use and value of the storyboards. It deals with the close relationship between the artist and director, drafts, and revisions. We then move onto the set, where we experience how the crew uses the boards to make the film come to life.

In addition, we have provided a DVD that includes the finished short film and some featured extras. These additional resources compare aspects of the project from script to screen.

PART 1

THE STORYBOARD

FIGURE P01. A storyboard frame with scene and shot numbers.

CHAPTER 1

A brief background on storyboards

CHAPTER 2

Producing storyboards

A brief background on storyboards

OVERVIEW AND LEARNING OBJECTIVES

In this chapter:

- 1.1 - What Are Storyboards?
- 1.2 - Is There Only One Type of Storyboard?
- 1.3 - Why Use Them? What Makes Them Important?
- 1.4 - What Is Portrayed in a Storyboard?
- 1.5 - Are Storyboards Different for Animated Movies or Computer Games?
- 1.6 - How Are Storyboards Evolving for the Future?

1.1 - What are storyboards?

Storyboards are a visual representation of the written word and a means to communicate, through images, what those words describe. Drawn in a series of frames, the pictures are used by movie directors and game developers to visualize physically their ideas and to determine whether or not they effectively tell the story. Boards enable movie and game creators to view and define a particular scene.

Consider a storyboard to be a visual road map to a script, shoot, or development process. Where it otherwise might take lines of text to describe camera motion or the positioning of objects within the scene, it will take just a glance at a storyboard to convey the same information. This enables filmmakers or game developers to visualize shots and scenes before the shooting begins.

Each storyboard displays a number of frames on the page that function as a window to the eye of the camera. What is detailed within the scene is detailed in the storyboard *frame*.

BRIEF REVIEW OF TERMS:

STORYBOARD A series of drawings, illustrations, or photographs that conveys a story or sequence of events and sometimes includes dialogue.

FRAME The viewing area as seen by the camera lens.

In essence, when looking at the frames of the storyboard, the viewer is seeing what will be viewed through the lens of the camera. Inside the frames are the objects that are depicted in the scene. Objects could include the actors, sets, and props.

NOTE *The number of frames per storyboard page varies with the artist, director, and aspect ratio of the camera, however, three frames per page is common.*

Let's take a look at an example of lines of text from the script of the film project *Overtime*, along with the corresponding storyboard (Figures 1.1-1 and 1.1-2).

Comparing the lines of text from the script with the storyboard page, we see that the objects within the frame and the camera movements are shown in greater detail on the storyboard than they are described in the script.

FADE IN:

EXT. QUIET CITY STREET - DAY

RACHEL (32) looks a bit out of place as a phone repair worker, with sunglasses and a wig but she walks around with a sense of purpose.

FIGURE 1.1-1. Part of the script for the short-film project *Overtime*.

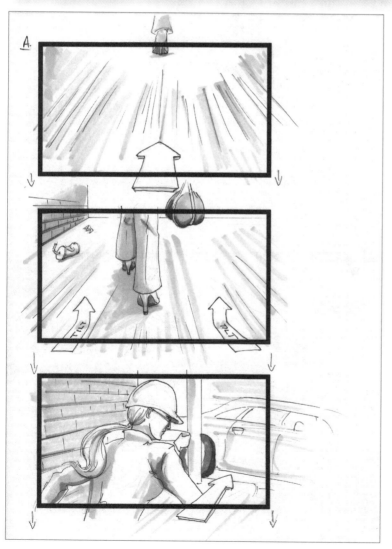

FIGURE 1.1-2. A storyboard from the short-film project *Overtime*. The full short film is included on the companion DVD.

A director or a group of creators in preproduction will have to translate the style and overall feel of the project from the text of the script into visual elements. This is where the storyboard process begins.

As the old Chinese proverb *"One picture is worth ten thousand words"* suggests, it would take several lines of text to describe the object action, camera movement, and style of the shot. For example, let's take one frame (Figure 1.1-3) from the storyboard and describe all of the style and movement depicted within the frame:

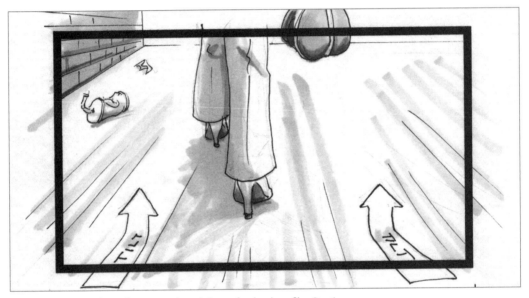

FIGURE 1.1-3. One frame from a storyboard drawn for the short film *Overtime.*

```
The camera will follow the object, RACHEL,
from a low angle, showing just her high
heels, then will tilt up to show her phone-
repair clothes and tools. The street will
be empty and there will be a building to
her left which she passes as she walks by
quickly.
```

This storyboard frame is relatively simple but a full paragraph of text is necessary to explain it. With additional complex camera movements and props, the description would extend to multiple paragraphs.

FIGURE 1.1-4. These four frames are taken from different storyboards. Each uses arrows as graphic elements to represent object or camera movement. The upper-left frame shows a dolly and zoom effect. The upper right shows the camera as it swings down on a boom. In the lower left the camera is performing a pan. In the lower right the arrows indicate the movement of the actor and the camera.

Arrows and other design elements are used to give the viewer a sense of motion (Figure 1.1-4). They indicate the desired camera movement, angle, and special effect.

Storyboards are a powerful tool for both preproduction and production. While in preproduction, storyboards make it possible for the director to visualize a scene coming to life. Shot sequences, camera setups, and object positioning can be worked and re-worked until the storyboard frames are functional, representing the director's vision and depicting the written story.

During production the boards act as a road map to the scenes being shot. For example, the crew members use the boards to construct a daily schedule or to set up a shot, and the director uses them to track the coverage of a scene, based on the original concepts.

We will examine why this is important and what is portrayed in the storyboards in the following sections.

1.2 - Is there only one type of storyboard?

As discussed in Section 1.1, a storyboard is a series of drawings that convey a story or series of events. Sometimes the illustrations are photographs and occasionally dialogue is included. In this book, we will cover one style of storyboard known as the editorial or production board. This type of board focuses on storytelling and camera movements. Different media use various types of art boards. Though the goal of streamlining communication and production does not change, the detail and methods of production might. For example, television commercials often require more detail and might show only a segment of the story. Computer games will use storyboards for mapping out the game play. Following are a few types of boards:

Editorial or production boards

Editorial and production boards tell a story and are sometimes a drawn translation of scripts. They reflect the director's or development team's ideas about the story and the camera shots.

Concept boards

Concept boards are very detailed illustrations that focus on the location, set, background scenery, or a dramatic event.

Commercial boards

Commercial boards are normally in color on large sheets of paper and are very detailed. Occasionally they are designed by advertising agencies for their clients.

Graphic novel or comic-book boards

Graphic novel and comic book boards are very similar to the editorial and production boards but are more detailed. They are not a stepping stone for production into moving images; therefore they do not include directions for camera movements.

Gameplay boards

Gameplay boards are used to map out the computer game players' actions and their available choices and reactions to the decisions made throughout the game.

Web site navigation boards

Web site navigation boards are thumbnails that create connections and aid in navigation of a Web site. The animation of the site can be illustrated.

Following is an interview with Beth Galton, a director of television commercials. Beth shares some insight about the practical use of storyboards.

A DIRECTOR'S USE OF STORYBOARDS　　　　**INTERVIEW**

Beth Galton

Director for ARF&CO

ST: Do storyboards reflect your vision of the script?

BG: I usually get a storyboard and script from the agency to bid on. Once I get the job, I will redraw the board using their initial ideas and add my additional thoughts as to how the copy and imagery could work together. I generally find I greatly expand their thoughts.

ST: Do you meet with the storyboard artist and talk about the script? If so, how many meeting and revisions are common?

BG: I usually work with them for the day. We meet in the morning and they look at my ideas and drawings and redraw the board so my thoughts are drawn more clearly. Most times they complete this process in one day.

ST: What do you like to discuss in the meeting to best represent what you are looking for in the boards? How much is your vision and how much is their artistic creativity?

BG: I like to discuss camera movement, and the action that is happening within the frame. By the time this is happening, I am usually pretty clear as to what and how I want the action drawn. The artist generally takes my terrible drawings and makes them come alive.

ST: How do storyboards help with your communication to your cast and crew?

BG: They give the crew and cast a good idea as to what I am looking for. It is a great tool for us to discuss the direction of each scene/set-up. The assistant director (AD) quite often cuts it up and posts it on a board so we keep track of each scene and have a visual reference of what we need to accomplish during the day. (As well as cross off so we know where we are.) We rarely have a script person unless there is talent or a complicated spot where timing is important.

1.3 - Why use storyboards? What makes them Important?

Storyboards have two main functions: first, to illustrate through a visual outline the director's conceptualization of a script. This is done in order to determine if the director's ideas are effective and to gather them into a central area. Second, the storyboard serves as a tool for the project. It becomes a reference guide for the director's vision, mapped out for the cast and crew in preproduction and during the shoot.

First: the director's vision

The end goal for any storyboard is to communicate a story and to make sure everyone involved in the creation of that story has the same understanding of what the vision is. This is important because crew members and cast have different backgrounds and perspectives, which could lead to different visions of the same text. For example, if you read the line:

```
The dog ran past the tree.
```

What type of dog did you visualize? What type of tree? What direction did you have the dog coming from?

FIGURE 1.3-1. A drawing of the line "The dog ran past the tree."

Chances are, your imagination created a scene different from the drawing (Figure 1.3-1) and different from that of other readers of this book. It is because of these differences in perspective that directors need to define how they are visualizing a script.

Now, let's take a look at a line of text from the script of the project *Overtime:*

```
Michele strides to the bar, standing next
to the Man without being recognized.
```

We can ask the same type of questions. What type of bar? What is she wearing? Where did she stride from? Is she standing to the right or to the left of the Man?

FIGURE 1.3-2. A storyboard scetch of the line "Michele strides to the bar, standing next to the Man — without being recognized".

All of these questions can be answered with just a glance at the storyboard frame, which is what makes a storyboard a great communication tool (Figure 1.3-2).

A director will read a script and ask these types of questions while developing an idea of how the story will be told. This is the first step in creating the storyboards. Emotion, imagery, and overall message, coupled with camera movements and shot sequences will be part of how the director tells the story.

Some directors like to sketch their own storyboards at this stage in order to help them streamline their ideas of the script. Other directors might call in an artist to try to capture the style and describe the ideas visually. The artist will then research the style the director is looking for to try to represent the director's concept in the storyboards.

A storyboard artist can research the style the director wants by watching related movies, analyzing graphic designs and photographs, and going to actual locations.

Directors will be able to visualize how the story develops through the storyboards' frames. Based on what they see, directors can make editorial modifications and adjustments to camera shot sequences until they are satisfied with how the story is being depicted.

Second: reference guide

As well as creating a clear image for people to visualize and comprehend a scene, a storyboard is a single point of reference where cast and crew can be assured of availing themselves of the same information (Figure 1.3-3).

FIGURE 1.3-3. A director and a director of photography talking on set about a shot, using the storyboards as a reference.

Storyboards are an important tool for saving time and money during the shoot. Sets can be a whirlwind of motion, changes, and confusion. It is often said that *"making movies is an exercise in Murphy's Law."* If proper preproduction has been done, and you have a clear storyboard, it will act as a "shot map" to keep you on the correct road. You will not get lost in the storm.

By this point in production, the sequencing is, for the most part, to the director's satisfaction, and the boards are used as a visual reference for upcoming shots or as a shot list. Storyboard frames can be crossed off once the director is satisfied with a particular shot. Sometimes, because of budget, weather, or actor availability, the shooting schedule might need to be rearranged. Having storyboards distributed to cast and crew helps everyone in the production to readjust to any changes there might be.

The following quote from director Nick Noyes describes using storyboards as a communication tool and as a reference guide:

NICK NOYES - DIRECTOR   QUOTE

Storyboards help a lot in preproduction. They really help show the director of photography (DP) what I want in each shot. On set they help me when it comes to knowing what I want. Everything is just a lot clearer in my head.

Storyboards are another step for you to really get to know your footage. It is a way to become aware of problems before you're on set, and helps you to fully understand what you want to shoot. For low-budget films, knowing your film and what footage you want is the best way to save money. If I am fully confident in what I want to film and what I do not need, it will save me money. All sets are stressful, and the better I know my film, the less confusion there will be, which will save the production time and money. When I get to the edit, I will not be missing any shots that I know I wanted, and it will help with a less "creative" edit to cover the holes I have. Again this will help me save money. People tend to get too excited and want to start to put images on tape, and forget about the importance of preproduction.

Types of scenes that should be storyboarded

It is beneficial for the entire script to be storyboarded. Even quick thumbnails can help clarify sequences. Outside factors such as time and budget, however, might make it impractical for any scenes other than the more complicated or expensive scenes to be boarded. Some of these scenes could have special effects (SFX), visual effects (VFX), stunts, and complex camera setups. The last thing any production needs is to waste time, money, and effort for a shot that is not working. Scrambling to figure out a shot or scene while on set is not desirable, especially if the problem could have been solved in preproduction with a storyboard. See Chapter 5 for more information on the use of storyboards and visual effects.

1.4 - What is portrayed in a storyboard?

Before we outline what is drawn inside and outside the storyboard frame, we need to look at how the page is constructed and the type of information that should be conveyed.

Anatomy of a storyboard

1. Number of the scene (SC)

2. Letter (or number) of the shot

3. Camera frame

4. Shows the shot continues to the next frame

5. Arrow shows camera movement

6. Arrow shows the subject movement

7. Subjects to be filmed in the camera frame

8. Area for continuation of action and notes

 It is good practice to have preprinted frames of different sizes to enable faster production of the storyboards.

The storyboard page shown in Figure 1.4-1 has three frames representing the camera's views. The size of the storyboard frame is equivalent to the camera frame (see Section 2.3). It is a typical storyboard on an 8.5x11 page with a 1.78:1 (high definition) *aspect ratio*.

The beginning of each scene is initialed in the top left of the page. The shot letter (or number) is marked at the upper left of each frame. If a shot is con-

> **BRIEF REVIEW OF TERMS:**
>
> **ASPECT RATIO** The aspect ratio is determined by the relationship of the height of the frame to its width.

tinued onto the next frame, then small arrows to the right and left side are drawn connecting the two frames.

The items within the frame are known as objects and subjects. Arrows within the frames show both camera and subject movements.

Figure 1.4-1 shows the type of information displayed on a storyboard.

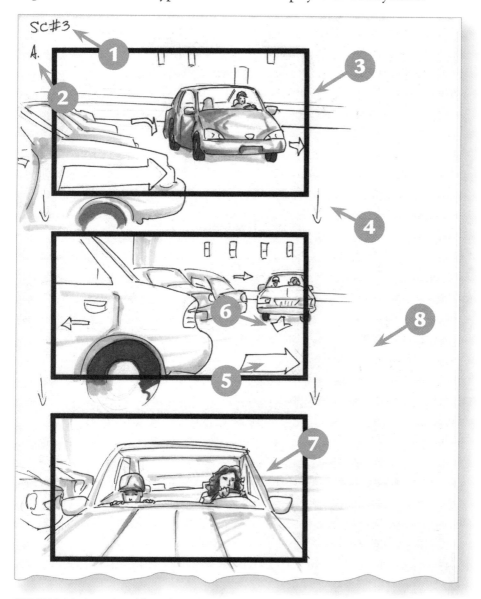

FIGURE 1.4-1. A storyboard from the project *Overtime.*

FIGURE 1.4-2. These images represent how the world or scene will look when using different aspect ratios. The photograph on the upper left is the full scene, and the image on the upper right shows what will be seen through the camera frame. The bottom two storyboards are the same scene, however one is using a widescreen and the other a high definition aspect ratio (see also Section 2.3).

Inside the storyboard frames

- Represents the aspect ratio of the camera

- Shows the objects and subjects that the camera will film

- Use of directional arrows represents camera and subject movement

Outside the storyboard frames

- The shot might continue between successive frames for complex camera work

- Shows continuation of action and additional information outside of the frame

- Director and script notes

- Scene and shot indicators

Seeing through the camera and storyboard frames

The purpose of filmmaking is to encourage an audience to understand a story from a particular perspective. A good director knows how to use composition, camera/subject movement, light, and focus in order to draw the viewer into a scene and have them perceive it the way the director envisioned it (Figure 1.4-2).

A good storyboard artist knows how to interpret the director's descriptions of a scene and draw them clearly so that the crew will be able to help the director produce what he has envisioned (Figure 1.4-3). In order to accomplish this, a good storyboard artist will have a firm understanding of filmmaking.

Framing for films is, in some ways, different than framing for other art forms. Many components make up the cinematic art form and have

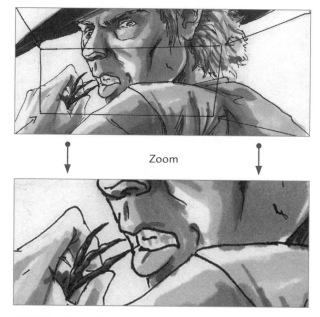

Zoom

FIGURE 1.4-3. With this frame, the storyboard artist drew a smaller frame inside the top image. This indicates a camera movement and an end point of that movement. The bottom frame shows how the shot will end.

FIGURE 1.4-4. Photograph of feet walking on a street.

an impact on how an image is perceived. For instance, consider the simple photograph of feet walking on a street (Figure 1.4-4).

In a film, this image would take on a different context when motion and sound reveal that the feet have paused because of hair-raising laughter coming from off-screen. This cannot easily be communicated in a photograph without perhaps altering the framing to include the person walking and the person laughing. Making that same change in the film might deflate the drama of the scene because the audience would immediately see the source of the laughter. Much of this has to be considered when making a film. The better the storyboard artist understands how to compose for films, the better the working relationship will be with the director. Storyboard artists who cannot quickly take in and accurately draw directions risk losing work to those who can.

In the following interview with storyboard artist Ryan D. Beckwith, several aspects of storyboard creation are revealed and discussed.

ST: What is your first step when handed a script and/or shot list?

RB: Rarely having a shot list, I typically only receive some combination of Director's treatment, agency scripts/boards, and perhaps an animatic. I usually go over the material very superficially at first, just to let it sink in, before going back over it in detail. Here, I am looking for imagery (what will I need to reference?), story (how would I frame this if left to my own devices?) and complexity. I am already beginning the calculus of budgeting my time.

ST: How does meeting with the director and or director of photography help with your preparation for the storyboards?

RB: I prefer to put as much responsibility for the boards on the director as I can. This is done entirely through exhaustive questioning and perhaps revisiting points a director is vague or unclear on, to pin him/her down on a decision. Details matter at this point. The director, faced with orchestrating a massive project, and responsible for thousands or millions of other peoples' dollars, is not worrying about which hand the model uses to pick up the detergent.

ST: What information is valuable to have when starting? Are there any potential problems to watch out for?

RB: In many commercial productions, final details are fluid, with changing actors, locations, scripts, etc. Trying to establish what is finalized (that which must be drawn specifically), and what can be left ambiguous is important. For details that are finalized, I will ask to be provided with headshots (for casting) or photos (location or products). These are almost universally available and the production staff is always happy to provide them. Beyond that I always expect changes. The punches to be rolled with will come.

ST: How much of the boards is your artistic creativity and how much is the director's?

RB: This varies dramatically from job to job. By rights I deserve a director's credit for some of the commercials I have boarded. On the other hand, I have had every independent thought overruled by a particularly involved director. In all cases I have the freedom of line, value, and expression of drawing, which is not to be underestimated, even in the most confining assignment.

1.5 - Are storyboards different for animated movies or computer games?

Storyboards are just as important, and their function for both animated films and computer games' cutscenes is very similar to that for traditional film-making. In preproduction, the story will have to be translated into a visual road map for motion, and the same creative process as for traditional movies is followed.

In production, the storyboard might acquire a more significant role for the *animators*. The storyboards are used as a foundation on which to develop a more detailed animation in 2D or 3D. A director for a traditional movie has the advantage of watching the acting of the cast or seeing the set and can make changes during shooting. Animated movies or computer games rely more on the storyboard drawings. Advances in technology, such as the use of *motion capture* and storyboard software, are increasing the detail and realism animators have available to them before real animation starts.

Animated movies

Animated movies also begin with a story. They might be developed from a script or from individual drawings. The storyboard will show an early representation of the characters and style. The boarded scenes might include greater detail, such as defined emotion and backgrounds, to build a stronger foundation for the creation of the real animation. Because of this, the storyboards for animated films are comparable to a production plan more so than those used for a traditional movie.

BRIEF REVIEW OF TERMS:

ANIMATION The techniques used to simulate motion through creating frames individually and then editing them as one sequence.

ANIMATOR One who creates animation.

ANIMATIC Images of a storyboard or still photographs edited in a sequence and synchronized with a soundtrack.

MOTION CAPTURE The process of capturing movement and translating the information into a digital form or model.

Storyboards are also used for animatics in creating animated movies. Ordinarily, an *animatic* combines images of the storyboard with the soundtrack. This allows the development team to work on the flow of the script, storyboard, and soundtrack. See Chapter 5 for more information on animatics.

In an interview with Kevin O'Hara, lead game designer for Sony Online Entertainment, we gain more insight about the use of storyboards in game development.

INTERVIEW

STORYBOARDS IN GAME DEVELOPMENT
Kevin O'Hara

Lead Game Designer, Sony Online Entertainment

ST: Computer games are getting more detailed in their cutscenes and in-game engine rendering acting like film scenes. How do storyboards enhance the development of the action in these scenes?

KH: With cutscenes, it acts exactly like it does in film production. It allows the artists to fully realize the action and framing before committing resources to creation and rendering of digital art assets.

ST: Were the storyboards hand drawn or did the artist use software or the game engine?

KH: It depends on the artist. Of the ones I've worked with, most would "hand draw" on the computer using a tablet. This allowed for quick revisions without annoying eraser dust. One storyboard artist who had worked in film before video games did his storyboarding on paper. The only advantage of that, other than it was in his comfort level, was he could come to meetings and sketch while the designers brainstormed ideas.

ST: In films, storyboard artists draw their boards from a shot list and script. Is it the same for computer games? If not, what is the process?

KH: For cutscenes, it usually follows a shot list and script. For gameplay, it is usually more from brainstorm sessions, though I would tend to write a script as well from the sessions to help the artists, because film production is my background.

ST: Where do you see the future of storyboarding for computer games?

KH: I feel they will be used increasingly as Hollywood becomes more involved in games and as designers understand the value of framing, pacing, and emotional impact. However, the majority of games will be made without storyboards for some time to come as many development companies don't understand the benefits or are not used to using them. Dedicated storyboard artists will still be uncommon for quite a while outside of third party companies that specialize in cutscenes such as Blur.

Computer games

Today's computer games are increasing in complexity, graphic capability, and powerful *game engines*. Games will use *gameplay boards* for user interaction and editorial or production storyboards for their cinematic or cutscenes. It is important to differentiate the production of the gameplay from the movie-like *cutscenes*. The gameplay of the computer game is the interaction the player has with the game.

Generally, the cinematic or noninteractive cutscenes are similar to mini movies and are not controlled by the player. These movies might be part of the introduction, ending sequence, or within the play of the game. The storyboards for these cutscenes are similar to those for traditional movies because they tell a story, show what the viewer will see, and describe the type of camera shots. After the storyboards are drawn, a development team will then create the sequence.

BRIEF REVIEW OF TERMS:

CUTSCENE The cinematic, generally noninteractive mini-movie sequences in video games. Most cutscenes stop the game play to advance the plot of the story.

GAME ENGINE The software designed for the creation and development of computer games.

GAMEPLAY The interaction the player has with the computer game.

GAMEPLAY BOARDS The map of actions and paths available to the player of a computer game throughout the course of a game.

With the advances of game engines, cutscenes are becoming increasingly integrated into the gameplay. Storyboards for these scenes might be utilized differently depending on the development team.

1.6 How are storyboards evolving for the future?

Although most storyboards are still primarily drawn by hand with pencil and paper, new trends are starting to become popular. High-powered computers, video cameras, and software are allowing more people to create their own movies for a fraction of what the cost of such an undertaking used to be. No matter the size of the movie, the use and advantages of storyboards does not change. New technology—both hardware and software—is increasing the ease with which storyboards can be made.

Hardware

As we will see in Chapter Five, one of the hardware advancements is that of graphic tablets and touch screens. Although graphic tablets have been used for some time, the development of these tablets into portable devices makes it easier for artists to bring their "workstations" with them anywhere. This allows artists to make quick changes to the storyboards on their computer while they are still in meetings or on set.

Software

Storyboarding software (also see Chapter Five) has advanced along with the computers running them. User-friendly boarding programs allow potential moviemakers to see their movie come to life before shooting, just as hand-drawn storyboards do. Movie-editing software now includes storyboard options for a complete preproduction, production, and postproduction package. Different software programs use various user interfaces; however, artistic ability is usually not a requirement. This allows a non-artist the ability to create detailed storyboards.

Types of computer-storyboarding software:
- FrameForge Previz Studio 3 by Innoventive Software, LLC
- SketchUp® Pro by Google
- Springboard by Six Mile Creek Systems, LLC.

- StoryBoard Artist Studio by PowerProduction Software

- StoryBoard Pro by Atomic Learning Inc.

- Storyboard Pro by Toon Boom Animation Inc.

For an in-depth list of computer software please see Chapter 5.

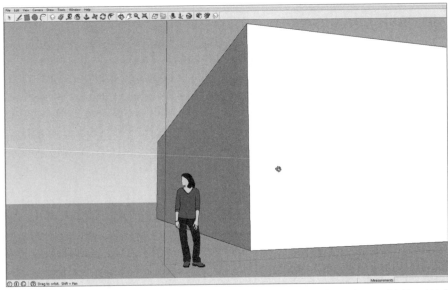

FIGURE 1.6. A screenshot taken of the beginning of a storyboard that is being drawn with SketchUp® by Google.

Alex Fernbach, a director and cameraman, describes the use of one of these programs in the following quote:

SUMMARY

Storyboards visually communicate the written word through a series of drawings quickly and effectively to be used by everyone in a film production. It is an important tool to save time and money during preproduction and production. There are many different types of storyboards and they can be very simple or very complex, depending on the director's needs. Storyboards are equally important and function in a similar manner for both animated films and computer games' cutscenes. Most storyboards are still drawn by hand with pencil and paper, but the use of computer software is becoming popular.

REVIEW QUESTIONS: CHAPTER 1

1. What are storyboards?

2. Is there only one type of storyboard?

3. Why use them? What makes them important?

4. What is portrayed in a storyboard?

5. How are storyboards different for animated films and computer games?

6. How have storyboards evolved and what will their future development be?

DISCUSSION / ESSAY QUESTIONS

1. Write an essay recalling the important information from the text and your thoughts concerning how to use the information.

2. Discuss and evaluate the storyboarding process.

3. Write about what you know about storyboarding and what you want to learn about storyboarding.

4. List the pro and cons of making storyboards.

5. Discuss any experience you might have filming or using storyboards.

1. Take a comic strip without the ending frame and draw the last frame using the concepts of storyboarding and your imagination.

2. Put a series of photographs or drawings in an order that will tell a story.

3. Identify and explain a page layout of this storyboard.

FIGURE EX-1. Use this, or another, storyboard to explain the page layout.

4. Take this photo and write a description.

FIGURE EX-2. Use this storyboard frame to write a description about an image.

5. Draw the text from the script *Mad Dash*, located on the DVD, into a storyboard page using the blank frames that are provided. Draw by hand (stick figures work) or use computer software. Extra blank frames and scripts are located in the back of this book.

```
MIKE (22) is sleeping in bed.

JENNIFER (21), Mike's wife, is sleeping
next to him in bed. She wakes up with a
fright and notices her alarm didn't go
off.  They are half-an-hour late getting
ready for work.
```

            JENNIFER
      Wake up! Wake up!
      Mike, we are late for
      work.

            MIKE

What! What did you say?

Blank storyboard frames for practice

FIGURE EX-3. Storyboard frames (2.39:1 widescreen) for practice drawing.

CHAPTER 2

Producing the Storyboards

OVERVIEW AND LEARNING OBJECTIVES

In this chapter:

- 2.1 - Where to start a storyboard project
- 2.2 - Who should be involved?
- 2.3 - What information needs to be gathered?
- 2.4 - Understanding the shot list
- 2.5 - Common types of camera shots
- 2.6 - Descriptions and examples of common camera shots
- 2.7 - How detailed do the storyboard drawings have to be?
- 2.8 - Who benefits from storyboards and why?

2.1 - Where to start a storyboard project?

Storyboard projects for film

Storyboarding is a process that begins with the script coupled with the director's interpretation of that text. We covered the way directors begin to break-down the script into visual images in Section 1.3. Now let's take a closer look at the process (Figure 2.1-1).

The filmmaking process begins many different ways. Studio executives generally acquire scripts and hire directors to bring them to the screen. Independent producers and directors often write or acquire a script based on their own ideas and look to find financing for it. The film student will have an assignment to fulfill and will craft a script to meet the requirements of their project. On occasion, the director might not even have a finished script before being inspired with ideas for a film. Regardless of how the project starts, the process is the same. The director's initial read of the script will spark her initial thoughts on style, tone, and how she would like to tell the story.

With additional review, the director will take notes on the script and possibly draw rough sketches or thumbnails to represent shots. These break-down elements begin to define the overall visual style of the film. Directors will then try to visualize types of camera angles, sizes, and movements, and shot sequences will emerge. The technical details might change in meetings throughout preproduction, especially with input from the director of photography, but at this stage these initial visual representations are needed in order to communicate the style and mood of the story the director is trying to tell. These descriptions are the building blocks of the shots and will translate into drawn storyboard frames.

NOTE

Storytelling is the essence of filmmaking. The job of the director is to tell the story as she conceptualizes it and to translate that vision for viewers to see. The handling of the script translation and the amount of input from crew members differ for each director depending on what seems to them to be the most effective way to tell the story.

Often research is done on the subject matter together with style and technical ideas. Sometimes the director is inspired by established works of art from a variety of types of media. Different locations will be scouted and sets will be built. Prop and wardrobe ideas will be conceived and gathered. Depending on the budget and the size of the production, a director might collaborate on ideas with crew members such as a production designer, or a costume designer. Ideas for casting the actors start to take shape. The location, prop, and talent photographs are taken, and overhead location diagrams are illustrated.

Storyboard development and use during the three phases of film creation

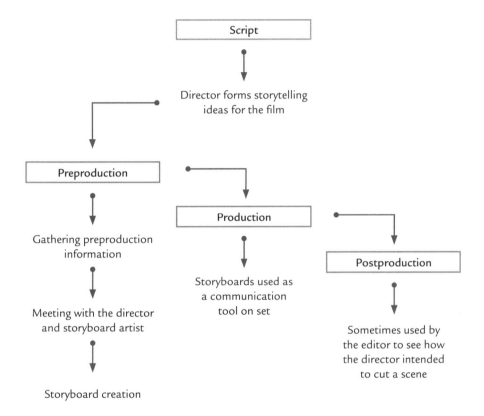

FIGURE 2.1-1. This figure outlines the steps of storyboard development and use. (The storyboard development and use for preproduction and production are further illustrated in Chapter 3 and Chapter 4. Storyboards are not normally needed in postproduction.)

As ideas start to solidify, the director may call a meeting, or a series of meetings, with the storyboard artist. The goal of these meetings is to effectively bring into focus and communicate the director's ideas. At this point, the story begins to come to life visually. The artist will ask questions about the scene, the objects within the scene, and how they interact with each other. How the meetings are run and the amount of collaboration from the storyboard artist or other crew members depends on the director. These meetings clarify how elements of the story will be portrayed so the storyboard artist can commence to draw the boards.

Let's revisit the script portrayal questions from the project *Overtime* example in Section 1.3, along with the line of text from the script.

```
Michele strides to the bar, standing next
to the Man without being recognized.
```

By just reading the line of text, the storyboard artist might have a very different concept of the scene than that of the director (Figure 2.1-2). The artist might see the bar as a night club that is dark and crowded rather than a pub or restaurant, or she might think the Man was distracted as Michele walks up to the bar in front of him. Which direction does she come from? What does she look like? The artist will have to ask these questions, and the director will have to create a dialog in order for the artist to understand what the director imagines. All the different objects and their interactions as detailed in each scene will have to be discussed.

Sample questions: What type of bar? What is Michele wearing? Where did she stride from? Is she standing to the right or to the left of the Man? What type of camera movement? How close are the shots going to be? What frame size should be used? Are there going to be any special props? What is the mood of the bar; dark and broody or light and crowded?

FIGURE 2.1-2. The storyboard frame for the script line "Michele strides to the bar, standing next to the Man – without being recognized."

Some of these questions, depending on the size of the project, could be answered from the location diagrams, props list, talent photographs, and the shot list. This information is all collected in preproduction.

Sometimes, to further clarify what is being discussed in the meeting, the storyboard artist will draw a quick stick-figure sketch of a shot or scene so the director can be sure they are on the same page. Once the director is confident that the artist understands the scene, the storyboard artist will do rough boards, quick sketches for each shot, so the director can see how the scene is working. For example, the director will be able to see if a particular shot works better as a high versus a low camera angle. Once preproduction is completed, the production phase can begin. On set, the storyboards are used as a communication tool by the director among the rest of the cast and crew.

The following is a quote from artist Ryan D. Beckwith regarding his experience in preproduction meetings.

QUOTE

RYAN D. BECKWITH - STORYBOARD ARTIST

I put preference on building a firm shot list (sketching and taking notes throughout) and establishing a shooting style (angles, framing, and mood). With luck, by the end of the meeting I have not just prepared, I have already begun.

Storyboard projects for video games

The starting point for a video game project could be a little different. The mini-movie cutscenes would be very similar to the filming method and would begin essentially from the director's or development team's initial conceptualization. Sometimes these cutscenes are completely different from the game style, however, and serve as separate short films.

Cutscenes are increasingly being integrated into actual gameplay, however. With the cutscenes as part of the overall game, many of the preproduction questions are answered from the outset. Development teams would already have made decisions about the type of overall style, look of the characters, use of lighting, and camera angles.

For the overall game, the storytelling, style, shots, and scenes will drive the development, as in filmmaking; in addition, however, a game developer will be concerned with other factors, such as user involvement and gameplay. With the advancing technology in gaming engines and motion capture, the games themselves are becoming interactive movies. Either way, the job of the editorial storyboard artist does not change significantly. The artist will still need to gather the preproduction information such as the shot list, illustrations, and diagrams and will need to attend meetings with the development team or director.

2.2 - Who should be involved?

Production hierarchies and job titles can differ based on the region of the world where the artist is working. Although the organization of the production might differ, the basic task of the storyboard artist will be the same. There will always be a script that the project is based on, and there will always be a person translating the script: the director.

Because the director is the person who is responsible for translating the script, the director is the primary person with whom the storyboard artist will meet and interact. The storyboard artist might come into contact with other members of the crew, but this is extremely rare. The person having the greatest bearing on the artist is the one translating the script.

Normally, the higher the budget, the greater the number of people involved. In this instance a dedicated storyboard artist will be hired as part of the crew. On smaller budget projects, however, sometimes an artist is not affordable. In that case, usually the director will sketch the boards. If a storyboard artist is part of the crew, a meeting with the director will take place to discuss the director's ideas. This is most often an individual meeting.

Primary figures in the collaboration of storyboards

Director
A director is a person who controls the creative aspects of a project and instructs the cast and crew. This includes turning the script into images and sounds. The director is the mastermind of the project and creates the overall vision and style of the film. The storyboard artist will work with the director to translate the story into illustrated drawings.

Storyboard Artist
The artist drawing the storyboards might be a professional artist or a crew member taking on the role. Quick sketches and nonprofessional drawing can still be an effective communication tool; however, the more detail drawn in the boards, the more information they can convey.

Additional crew members involved in the storyboard creation

Filmmaking is a collaborative process. In order to be comprehensive, we will briefly discuss other members of the crew who may play a role during a storyboarding meeting. As stated above, these individuals will rarely interact creatively with the storyboard artist, but because productions vary it will benefit you to understand who the artist might encounter in the job field.

Possible members of the crew who might also be invited to a storyboarding meeting are the director of photography, production designer, or producer. Some directors work very closely with these crew members even while translating the script and crafting the shots.

Director of Photography

A director of photography is a movie photographer (cinematographer) who is in charge of shooting the movie and is responsible for achieving the director's vision through artistic and technical decisions related to the images.

Producer

A producer creates the conditions for making movies. The producer coordinates, supervises, and controls matters such as fund-raising, hiring key personnel, and arranging for distributors. The producer will interact with the storyboard artist somewhat, however, the role is usually more one of support.

Production Designer / Set Designer

A production designer is responsible for the overall look of the film's sets. The designer is the key artist of the production, charged with designing and dressing the space where a scene will be filmed. The designer works with the director and producer to create settings that conform to the visual style of the film. They will have schematics of the set, location images, and illustrations of special props. The storyboard artist will use these photographs and diagrams to help with the detail of the boards.

BRIEF REVIEW OF TERMS:

INDEPENDENT FILM / INDIE An independent film or "indie" film is produced outside of the Hollywood studio system.

MAJORS Motion pictures, normally with a large budget and significant size in scope.

SHORT FILM A film that is under 60 minutes in length.

2.3 - What information needs to be gathered?

Before storyboards can be created, information needs to be gathered. Time and budget issues might hinder the collection of all the different types of information on the list for a project, however, it is important to try and acquire as many of the list items as possible in order to create the most comprehensive boards.

- Script
- Shot list
- Location diagrams and overhead illustrations
- Talent and location photographs
- Prop and wardrobe illustrations and photographs
- Talks with the director and the storyboard artist
- Aspect ratio

Why is this list valuable to a storyboard artist?

To maximize the effectiveness of the storyboards and to contribute to adequate preproduction, an artist needs to draw each frame so that it closely resembles the intended image to be filmed. She must accurately portray what the camera will see before the production phase has even begun (Figure 2.3-1).

Script
The project starts with the script. It is a document that is specially formatted and contains the narrative to be filmed. This will provide the artist the overall story and a reference to the events.

Shot list
A shot list is a document detailing all of the intended shots for each scene. It includes a written description of each shot explaining camera view and movement, frame size, and character actions. The storyboard artist will work primarily from the shot list.

Location and set diagrams
Location diagrams are often overhead diagrams of the shooting area. These work as a map to place camera setups and track camera movements within the shot environment.

Talent and location photographs

Photographs of the actual actors and locations are a reference for the storyboard artist. With these she can draw the likeness of individual characters.

Prop and wardrobe illustrations and photographs

Props are objects that can be held or used by characters within a scene. Wardrobe is any piece of clothing or item worn by a character. Photographs or illustrations of any unique props or wardrobe items will help the storyboard artist capture the style of said objects in her drawings. Some productions might emphasize certain elements more so than other productions. For example, a science fiction movie might have very unique imagery that needs to be drawn.

Meetings with the director and storyboard artist

One of the major phases of preproduction is the refinement of the director's vision into definable images and styles. Every director is different, and each handles the preproduction process in their own way. The importance of clear and precise preproduction planning will save time, money, and a great deal of confusion once filming begins and can be achieved from a series of meetings with the director.

Aspect ratio

A storyboard artist should ask about the aspect ratio that is intended to be used during production. This will determine the actual frame size and allow the artist to closely capture what the camera will see on set.

Types of information used in preproduction for storyboard development

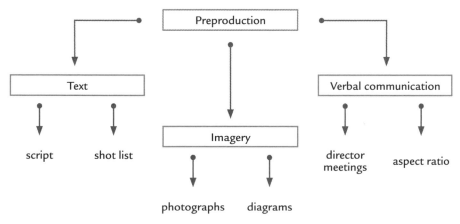

FIGURE 2.3-1. An illustration to highlight that the information gathered for storyboard development comes from different sources, media, and forms.

Aspect ratios

As we learned in Chapter 1, aspect ratio is determined by the relationship of the height of the frame to its width. The frame of the storyboard needs to proportionally match the ratio of the camera frame. This will allow the storyboard frame to accurately represent what the motion picture camera will see within its viewfinder when the cinematographer sets up a shot. Whereas consumer video cameras have fixed aspect ratios, professional motion picture cameras can be adjusted according to what the ultimate distribution format for the filmed media will be (Figure 2.3-2).

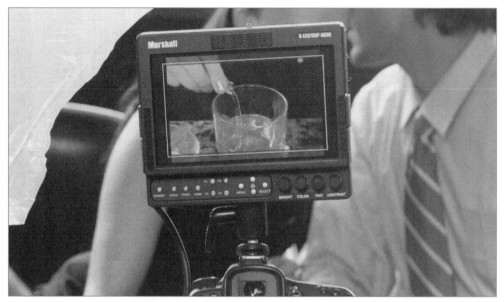

FIGURE 2.3-2. A photograph of a larger viewing screen for the Canon 7D camera shooting in 1.78, high definition.

For example an older television will have an aspect ratio of 1.33:1. The image on that television will appear relatively square. A new wide-screen television will use an aspect ratio of 1.78:1 and the image will be wider and will appear rectangular. Similarly, movie cameras can shoot in a multitude of aspect ratios. Movie theaters will adjust the width of their screens using curtains that retract, corresponding to the width of the film's ratio. Common aspect ratios in use for film and television are listed and illustrated for your reference (Figure 2.3-3 - Figure 2.3-8).

NOTE *Aspect ratios are usually shortened to leave out the "to 1," taking for granted they are always in relation to 1. 1.33:1 becomes 1.33. and 2.35:1 becomes 2.35.*

Common aspect ratios

1.33:1 - TV and computer screen
This ratio includes television and computer screens. It is also called 4:3 or Academy Standard.

1.66:1 - 16mm Film or European Projection
European standard and 16mm ratio.

1.78:1 - High definition
Video widescreen standard, used in high-definition television. It is also called 16:9.

1.85:1 - American Projection
American and United Kingdom widescreen standard for theatrical film and 35mm ratio.

2.39:1 - Widescreen, Super 35
This ratio includes 70 mm, Widescreen, Cinerama, CinemaScope, and other super widescreen formats.

1.43:1 - IMAX
70mm wide film, however the film runs through the camera and projector sideways. This allows for a physically larger area for each image.

BRIEF REVIEW OF TERMS:

16MM Sixteen millimeter refers to the width of the film. Sixteen millimeter filming gives a frame aspect ratio of 1.33: 1 and is considered an economical alternative to 35mm filmmaking.

35MM Thirty five millimeter filming gives a frame aspect ratio of 1.85: 1.

HIGH DEFINITION (HD) High definition refers to video having higher resolution than standard DEFINITION (SD) and is digitally broadcast using video compression.

An important question for the artist to ask is what aspect ratio is intended to be used during the filming of the production, in order that the storyboard frames will reflect the proportion of the camera frame.

FIGURE 2.3-3. 1.33 (4:3) – Television

FIGURE 2.3-4. 1.66 - 16mm Film or European Projection

FIGURE 2.3-5. 1.78:1 - High definition (16:9)

FIGURE 2.3-6. 1.85:1 - American Projection

FIGURE 2.3-7. 2.39:1 - Widescreen, Super 35

Drawing correct aspect ratios

A common configuration for storyboards is three frames per sheet of paper. The artist will use various sizes of paper based on the specifics of the job and her personal preference. The size and number of frames per sheet are dependent on the artist or the director. For example, a director might ask for only one frame per board if the artist is hired to draw only key frames. On other occasions, she might want more than ten frames in order to determine how complete scenes progress. Once the number of frames per page is chosen, the artist will then draw them in their proper aspect ratio.

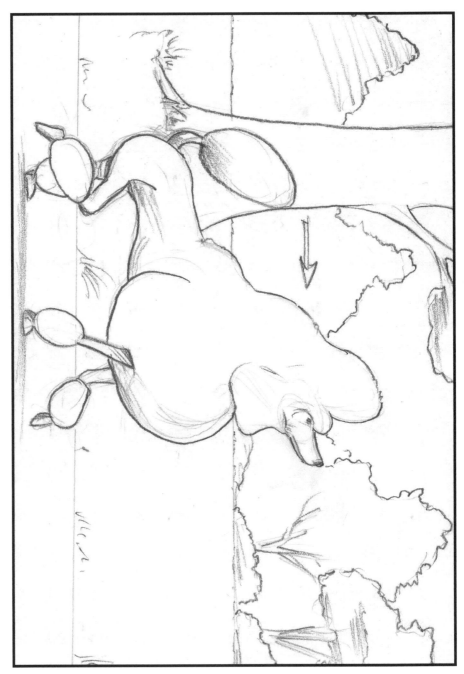

Fi*GURE 2.3-8.* IMAX – 1.43:1

To determine the proper aspect ratio for a frame this formula can be used:

h x a= w

Frame Height (h) times desired Aspect Ratio (a) equals the correct width (w).

Simply take the height of the desired frame and multiply it by the chosen aspect ratio that the boards will reflect. The artist will determine a height based on how large she wants the frame to be. For example, to fit three 1.66 aspect ratio storyboard frames onto an 8.5x11 inch page of paper, the desired height of each frame could be three inches. To produce a correct 1.66 aspect ratio for the frame being drawn, simply multiply 3 by 1.66. Rounding up, this will give a width of 5 inches.

3 x 1.66 = 4.98 (5)

Here is another example using a different height, but the same aspect ratio, 1.66. The resulting frame is illustrated in Figure 2.3-9. The height of 2 inches multiplied by 1.66 equals a width of 3.32.

2 x 1.66 = 3.32

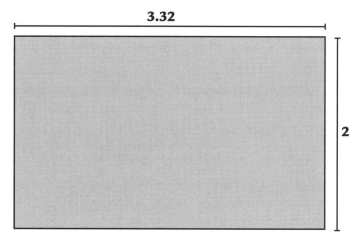

FIGURE 2.3-9. The fames is and examples of 2 x 1.66 = 3.32

2.4 - Understanding the shot list

To effectively depict a scene, the storyboard artist needs to understand composition, camera placement, and angles. She also must become familiar with illustrating movement. Camera shots can be divided into a few different categories dealing with the size, angle, and movement of the camera. There is also a category that classifies how a shot is used in editing to describe its effect on the storytelling of a scene. These components are utilized in the primary document the storyboard artist will reference: the shot list.

Translating the shot

The storyboard artist will need more information than can be gained by just reading the script. In section 2.1 we talked about the types of questions a storyboard artist might ask the director when first starting to capture the director's vision in the sketches for the frames. Many of those questions will begin to be answered by the shot list. It is important for the artist to understand the language that will be used to relate camera positioning and movement.

For example, take this line of text from a script:

> Michele strides to the bar, standing next
> to the Man without being recognized.

The director may decide to break down the line into a shot using this verbal description:

> "I want to start with a wide shot and then the camera will dolly in, then pan left and end up with a close-up of Michele."

That description would be written into the shot list and most likely appear in this form:

> WIDE SHOT- Camera dollies in, pans left and ends in a close-up (CU) of Michele as she strides into the bar.

The storyboard artist will have to be able to accurately translate the directions into a drawing. In order to do this, the artist needs to understand the terminology the director is using so she can draw the frame. In this one set of directions alone, the artist will have to comprehend and be able to draw a wide shot, dolly, pan, and close-up. A list of different camera shots is explained and drawn in Section 2.5.

Reading a shot list

Shot lists are generally organized in the same manner. Usually the scene number and sometimes a brief description are written as a header, then, all of the shots relating to that scene are placed underneath.

The shot description itself will generally follow a certain pattern. The size of the frame is usually written, followed by a brief description of the action the camera sees together with the camera's movement. When a shot contains camera movement, the final frame size is also described as well as what is being seen within the frame.

The assembly of a shot description will look like this:

> FRAME SIZE - Description of the action and camera movement, ending frame size and description of what is now seen.

The frame size is determined by how close the camera will be to the subject it is filming. The shot description should indicate the angle of the camera, but it might not always do so, and further elaboration might be necessary. The shot description will also indicate the camera and character movement.

Since most shot lists are written in shorthand, the artist will also need to understand how the terminology is abbreviated.

Here is another example from the script of *Overtime* using an abbreviated shot description from scene 4:

> SC#4 – EXT BAR – MOMENTS LATER
>
> B- MS (OTS) - Rachel drops into pass window. Tilt down to reveal wig and glasses.

The lines from the shot list translate into:

1. This shot is in scene 4

2. Location is outside of the bar

3. Shot B

4. A medium shot (MS) that is over the shoulder (OTS)

5. The character action is Rachel drops into passenger window.

6. The camera tilts down to show wig and glasses

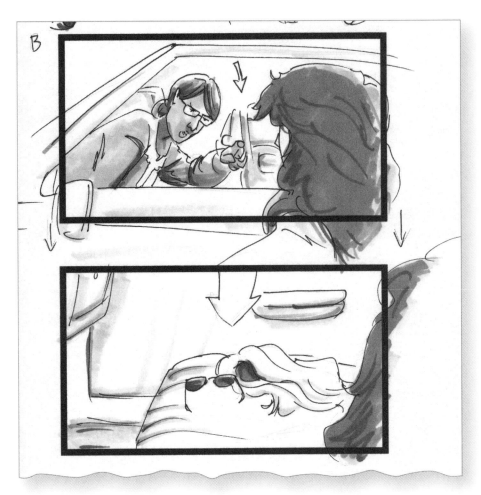

FIGURE 2.4-1. The storyboard frames for SC#4 – MS (OTS) - Rachel drops into pass window. Tilt down to reveal wig and glasses.

Figure 2.4-1 shows the corresponding storyboard for this shot. The B for the shot number is in the upper left corner. Arrows between the two frames indicate that these two frames are linked. The top frame shows the medium over-the-shoulder shot of the subject. An arrow above the subject's hand shows the action of the subject. In the lower frame, the larger arrow pointing downward represents the tilt camera movement and its direction.

NOTE

The artist will have to be able to draw three-dimensional action onto a two-dimensional page. To do this, arrows and other design elements are used to show the motion of the camera and the motion of the objects within the frame.

Drawing the frame

After understanding the director's intentions, the storyboard artist will now have to translate this onto paper. For example, in Figure 2.4-2 there is a sketch of a scene inside a bar. The shot calls for a wide shot of the interior with a man standing at the bar, while another character enters and takes a position next to him. Notice the frame seems to capture a wide area of the room. A man is shown standing at the bar while the second character enters. Her action is captured by drawing her twice, once to show her walking and another time to show where in the frame she will stop. Arrows are drawn to indicate the direction and path this character will take. The goal for both the double drawing of the character as well as the horizontal and the curved arrows is to communicate that the character will walk into the bar from the right of the frame to the left side and will stop around the corner of the bar.

FIGURE 2.4-2. The storyboard frame for Scene 5, shot A.

Figure 2.4-2 captures script direction from Scene 5, shot A from the film *Overtime* that reads:

> SC#5 – INT BAR- DAY - A- WS (MASTER)- Rachel walks
> up to bar as the Man orders a drink at bar.

BRIEF REVIEW OF TERMS:

EXTERIOR (EXT) A representation in visual art of the outdoors or a scene shot outside a studio.

INTERIOR (INT) The inside, a picture, or a rendering of a building or room.

OFF SCREEN (OS) The action or sound that takes place out of the frame of the camera.

2.5 - Common types of camera shots

A shot can be fit into a variety of categories including: scale, angle, movement, and editing segues. Listed are some common camera shots used for filming and creating storyboards. Most shots are executed with different combinations. For example, a master shot could be a wide shot, dolly, tracking, and a low angle. In the next few pages, the listed shots are explained and illustrated (Figures 2.6-1 through 2.6-13).

Field-size or scale

The field-size or scale grouping indicates how close or far away the object looks in the camera frame when being filmed. It is a proportion shot used to determine the dimensional relationship of the camera frame to objects it is capturing.

1. Close-Up (CU)
2. Extreme Close-Up (ECU)
3. Full or Figure Shot (FS)
4. Insert
5. Long Shot (LS)
6. Medium Shot (MS)
7. Single
8. Two Shot
9. Wide Shot (WS)

Camera placement or angles

The camera placement or angle category describes the directional relationship between the camera and the object it is viewing. These shots indicate the point of view of a camera from which the camera films a subject or scene.

1. Aerial Shot
2. Canted Frame
3. High Angle
4. Low Angle
5. Over the Shoulder (OTS)
6. Profile
7. Reverse Shot (Angle)
8. Straight On or Frontal

Camera movement

The camera movement category is any shot that changes the frame, perspective, or subject view, with the movement of the camera. Some scenes might take more than one storyboard frame to represent the action clearly. Combining storyboard frames to depict camera movement is a common method used to help closely translate the action onto the page.

1. Boom Shot
2. Car Mount
3. Crane Shot
4. Dolly Shot
5. Follow Shot
6. Hand-Held
7. Pan
8. Smash Zoom
9. Static Shot
10. Steadicam Shot
11. Swish Pan
12. Tilt
13. Tracking Shot
14. Traveling Shot
15. Zolly
16. Zoom

Editorial, editing, and point of view

In this category are types of shots that do not describe the camera placement, angle, or movement, but relate how the shot will be utilized for storytelling or editing purposes.

1. Cutaway
2. Establishing Shot
3. Freeze-Frame Shot
4. Jump Cut
5. Master Shot
6. Match Cut (Dissolve)
7. Objective Shot
8. Point-of-View Shot (POV)
9. Reaction Shot
10. Subjective Shot

Many camera shots are a combination of different shot categories. For example, an establishing shot could also be a panning long shot. In Figures 2.6-1 through 2.6-13 one element is pulled from the shot for further explanation.

2.6 - Descriptions and examples of common camera shots

Figure 2.6-1 shows camera shots from the field-size and scale category. The camera starts with the frame very close to the subject in an extreme close-up (ECU). It is so close that it shows only a small area of the field. In this case, it shows just the subject's eye. The camera then cuts to show more of the subject, but is still relatively close to the subject in a close-up (CU) shot. In the next frame, the camera cuts again to show a medium shot (MS).

Camera Field size or Scale Shots

Extreme Close-Up (ECU)
Extreme close-up is reserved for dramatic impact. The shot might show just the eyes of an individual.

Close-Up (CU)
A close-up framed shot is taken at close range when the subject is larger than the frame. On a person, the frame is often from the top of the head to the top of the chest.

Medium Shot (MS)
A medium shot is taken from a medium distance and normally from the waist up.

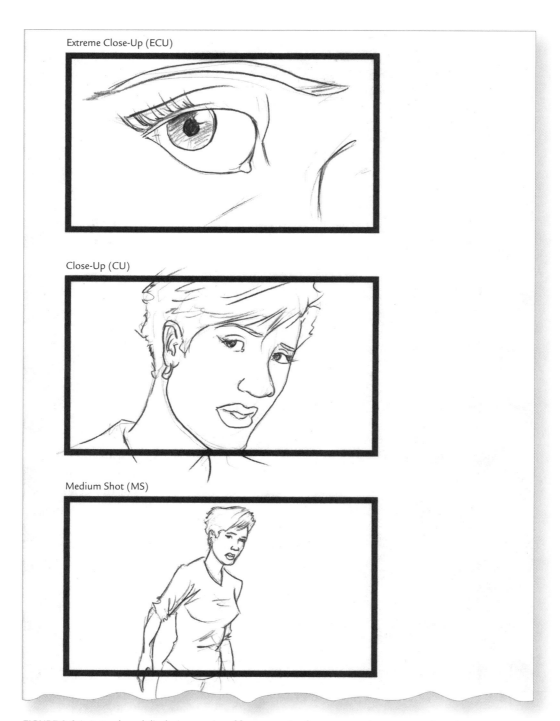

Extreme Close-Up (ECU)

Close-Up (CU)

Medium Shot (MS)

FIGURE 2.6-1. A storyboard displaying a series of frames ranging from extreme close-up to medium shot.

This storyboard sequence continues in the field-size and scale category. Figure 2.6-2 continues from Figure 2.6-1 with the camera cutting back further to reveal our subject fully. In this case, to show our subject from head to toe in a full or figure shot (FS).

In the next frame, the camera has continued to move back. Our subject is now revealed to be standing in front of a building in a long shot (LS).

NOTE   A full shot and long shot are sometimes interchangeable, depending on the other shots in the scene.

In our last storyboard frame in this sequence, the camera is out even further, for a wide shot. Now our subject is shown to be running away from a UFO.

Full or Figure Shot (FS)
A full shot sometimes is called a Long Shot (LS) and is taken where the frame captures the relative distance between the top of a person's head to their feet.

Long Shot (LS)
The long shot is sometimes called a full shot (FS) and is taken where the frame captures a broad view of the environment and away from the subject.

Wide Shot (WS)
A wide shot is taken from a distance and reveals where a scene is taking place.

Extreme Long Shot
The extreme long shot is a view from an even greater distance than a long shot (LS). Often people-sized objects are small within the frame.

BRIEF REVIEW OF TERMS:

FOREGROUND The foreground is part of a scene or picture that is nearest to and in front of the viewer.

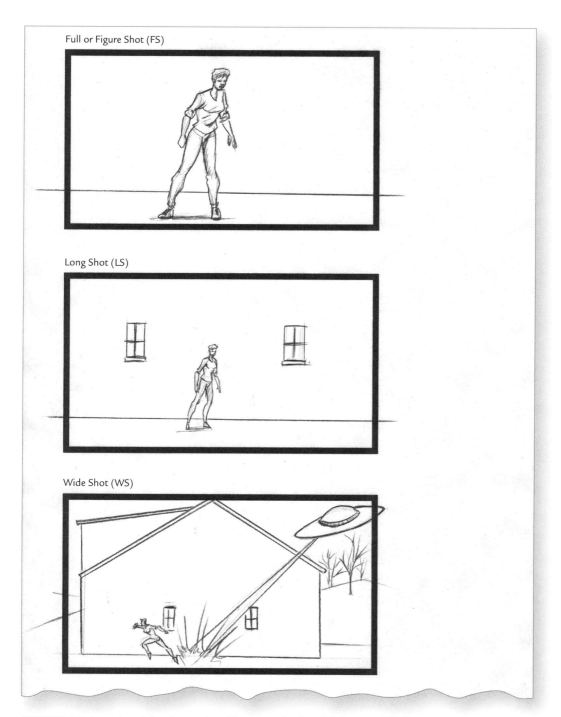

Full or Figure Shot (FS)

Long Shot (LS)

Wide Shot (WS)

FIGURE 2.6-2. A storyboard showing a series of frames ranging from full-figure to wide shot.

In this storyboard (Figure 2.6-3) the top frame is a two shot. Assuming this storyboard was part of a simple three-shot scene, and was the widest shot, this shot would be considered the master shot. The camera shifts in the next storyboard frame to a single shot with only one subject. Editorially, this frame is also a reaction shot; the subject's face registers quite a look of surprise.

The last shot is an insert shot and is the reason for the reaction displayed by the subject in the previous frame. Although the purse was previously shown, in the first two frames the camera did not show what was inside the purse. The insert shot covers the same subject, but from a different, closer angle.

Two Shot

A two shot is a frame that encompasses a view of two people or subjects. Many common two shots have one subject in the foreground and the other in the background.

Single

A single shot is a frame that encompasses a view of one person or subject.

Insert

An insert is a shot filmed that covers action already covered in the master shot, but from a different angle or focal length. It is generally used to clarify what was already seen.

NOTE

Figure 2.6-3 is an example of camera shots being a combination of multiple categories. The two-shot is also the master shot in this sequence and the single shot is also a reaction shot.

Two Shot

Single Shot also a Reaction Shot

Insert Shot

FIGURE 2.6-3. A storyboard showing a series of frames including a two, single, and insert shot.

This series of storyboard frames illustrates different camera angles (Figure 2.6-4). In the top frame the camera is placed above the subject and is looking down onto the subject. In the next frame, the camera is outside and goes to an even higher angle, the sky. In the last frame the camera is looking up to the subject from below the desk in a low-angle shot.

Camera-Placement or Angles Shots

High-Angle
A high-angle shot is the camera shot usually set above the eye line of the subject.

Aerial Shot
An aerial shot is an extreme high-angle shot that is usually done with a crane. It also can be done from airplanes and helicopters.

Low-Angle
A low-angle camera shot is usually below the eye line of the subject.

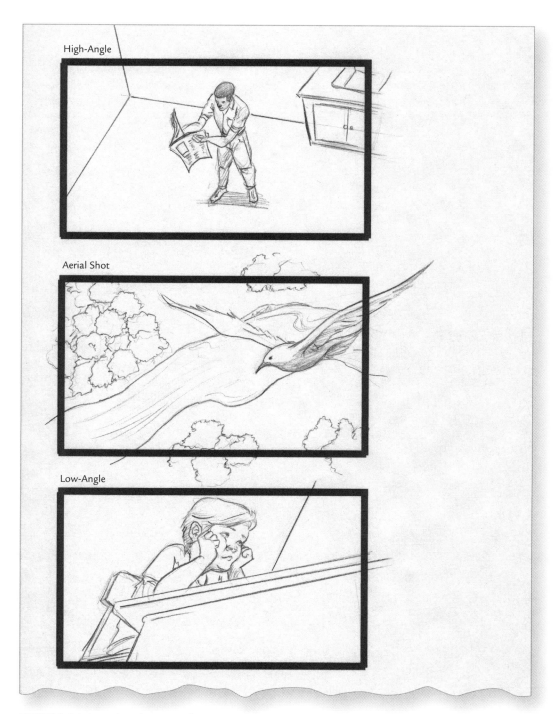

High-Angle

Aerial Shot

Low-Angle

FIGURE 2.6-4. A storyboard sequence illustrating camera angles from aerial to low.

In this storyboard, we continue to illustrate various camera angles (Figure 2.6-5). In the storyboard in Figure 2.6-4, we highlighted camera angles that are set up along a vertical axis. This set of frames will highlight angles that are set up along a horizontal axis. The first frame shows a profile or side view of the subject. In the next frame, the camera is moved in front of the subject. In the last frame, the camera views the subject over the shoulder of another subject, which shows the man standing in front of another person.

Profile
A profile is a side view of an object or structure, especially of the human head.

Straight On or Frontal
A straight-on is a non-angled view of the subject in the frame.

Over the Shoulder Shot (OTS)
The over-the-shoulder shot is a view of someone or something taken from over the shoulder of another person. The back of the shoulder and head of this person is used to frame the image of whatever or whomever the camera is pointing toward.

Profile

Straight On or Frontal

Over the Shoulder Shot (OTS)

FIGURE 2.6-5. A storyboard showing camera angles around a subject.

The first frame on this board is the reverse shot from the over-the-shoulder shot from the storyboard shown in Figure 2.6-6. The camera has now changed the angle to show the subject whose shoulder was viewed in the last frame. We see whom the man was talking to. The middle frame shows the two subjects turning away from the camera, with the angle of the camera tilted to one side in a slight diagonal.

Reverse Shot or Reverse Angle
A shot that views the action from the opposite side of the previous shot.

Canted Frame
A canted frame is also known as a Dutch angle and is a shot that is tilted 25 to 45 degrees to one side, causing horizontal lines be at an angle.

BRIEF REVIEW OF TERMS:

DUTCH TILT, DUTCH ANGLE The Dutch tilt/Dutch angle is also known as a Canted Frame and is a shot that is tilted 25 to 45 degrees to one side, causing horizontal lines be at an angle.

The last frame on this board is a movement shot. The camera will move to or around a subject. What makes this shot a dolly shot is that the camera will be placed onto a moving platform. This allows the camera to move smoothly.

Camera movement shots

Dolly Shot
A dolly is a platform that enables a movie or video camera to move during shots. This shot is part of the camera movement category.

FIGURE 2.6-6. A storyboard showing both camera movement and camera angles.

This sequence of frames continues the camera-movement shots (Figure 2.6-7). In the first frame, there is an arrow indicating the movement of the camera. In a tilt, the placement of the camera remains the same, but the body of the camera is rotated up or down. In this case it is rotated up.

Both the boom and the crane shot are high-angle shots with the camera being attached to a boom or crane. This allows the camera to move freely as if it was floating in the air. In the middle frame, the boom shot is used indoors.

In the last frame, the arrows indicate the camera movement and the smaller box drawn around the subject indicates the start location of the camera before the movement.

Tilt / Tilting
A tilt or tilting is a cinematographic technique by which the camera rotates up or down.

Boom Shot
A boom shot is also called a jib shot, and refers to a high-angle shot, sometimes with the camera moving. For this type of shot, the camera is mounted onto a boom.

Crane Shot
A crane shot is taken by a camera mounted on a crane and is often used for shots that view the scene from above or to move the camera into or away from a subject.

FIGURE 2.6-7. A storyboard sequence with camera rotation and changes in positioning.

This set of frames (Figure 2.6-8) demonstrates camera and subject movement. The top frame shows a view from the camera mounted on a car looking back toward the driver. The next frame portrays a view from a static camera, with the subject watching a police car speed across the frame. Once the car has raced by, the camera moves with the subject as she walks across the road. Unlike the dolly shot shown with Figure 2.6-6, the camera on a steadicam shot is not fixed on a platform, rather it is an apparatus that decreases the shake of the hands when the camera is held while shooting.

Car Mount

Car-mount shots are taken by a camera that is mounted on an automobile or other type of vehicle.

Static Shot

In the static shot, the camera and frame do not move when shooting.

Steadicam Shot

A steadicam shot uses an arm and harness to mount the camera to the operator's body, allowing for steady camera movement without a track. The steadicam also enables the camera to travel in areas where a dolly with a track could not, such as a street with live traffic traveling on the road.

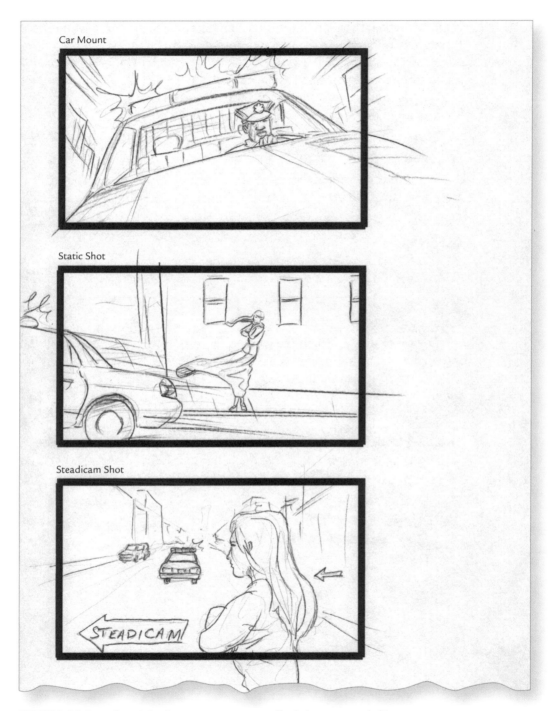

FIGURE 2.6-8. A storyboard showing camera movements of both the camera and objects.

In this storyboard (Figure 2.6-9), the camera is making a series of motions. In the first frame, the camera is moving horizontally to show more of the canyon. Pans can move left or right at various speeds. The next storyboard frame showcases a pan that is so fast the detail in the camera frame cannot be observed until it rests on its subject. In the last frame, the camera is moving with a subject, keeping the frame on that subject.

Pan
A pan is to move a camera laterally left or right to follow an object or to create a panoramic effect.

Swish Pan
A swish pan is a panning shot in which the scene moves too quickly to be observed until it rests on its subject.

Whip Pan
A type of pan shot in which the camera moves sideways so quickly that the picture blurs into indistinct streaks. It is commonly used as a transition between shots, and can indicate the passage of time and/or a frenetic pace of action.

Tracking Shot
A tracking shot is when the camera is being moved by means of wheels, as on a dolly.

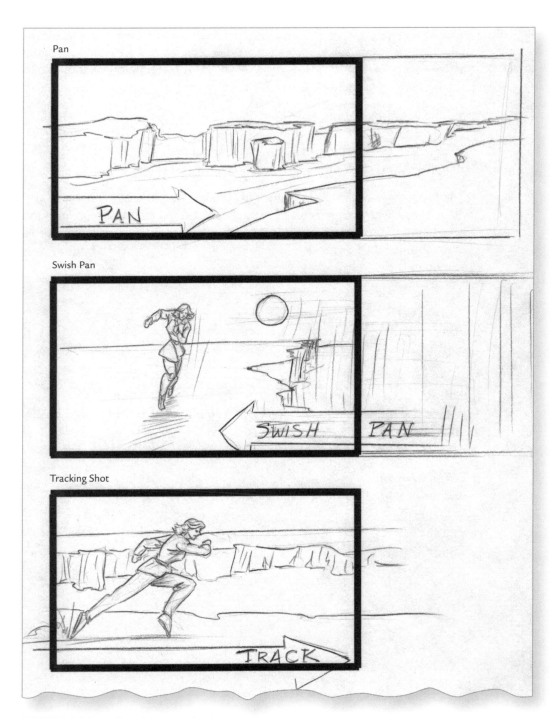

FIGURE 2.6-9. A storyboard sequence showing camera movement.

The storyboard frames represented in Figure 2.6-10 show camera movement into or away from the subject. In the first frame, the camera is static and the cameraman increases or decreases the focal length of the lens to move the camera frame closer or farther away from the subject.

A zolly is drawn in the next frame; it displays the use of a combination of a dolly and a zoom moving in opposite directions. In this example, the box around the subject indicates where the camera frame will end after the zoom, and the arrow shows the direction of the movement of the dolly.

The last frame is the smash zoom. This is a very quick zoom—in this example, into the werewolf's eye. Again, the smaller tilted box drawn on an angle represents where the camera frame will stop on the zoom. The camera shots in this frame add a dramatic effect for the viewer to appreciate the transformation of the werewolf.

Zoom
Zoom gradually changes the focal length of the lens. It gives the effect of dollying in or out without moving the camera.

Zolly
Zolly is a shot involving a dolly and zoom combination. Ordinarily, the dolly and zoom are moving in opposite directions.

Smash Zoom
A smash zoom performs the dolly zoom effect very quickly.

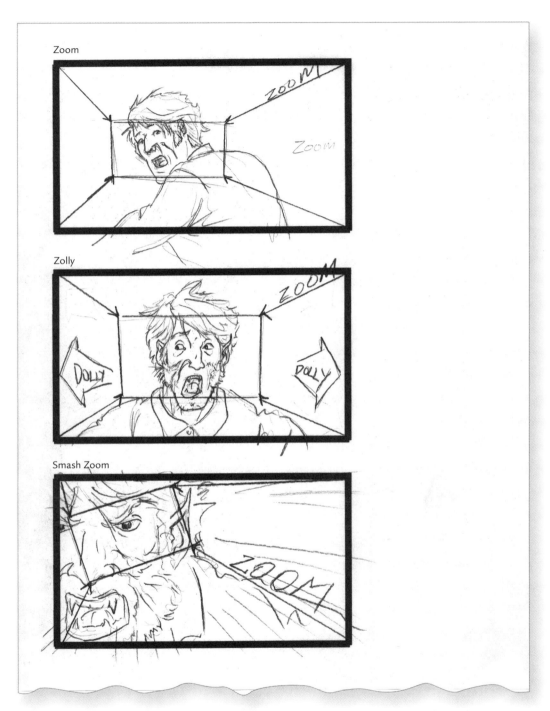

Zoom

Zolly

Smash Zoom

FIGURE 2.6-10. A storyboard sequence showing multiple camera frames. The start position and the end position after the camera movement.

The first frame on this board (Figure 2.6-11) is a following shot. The camera position does not move but it follows the subject's movement. In this case, the camera follows the werewolf as he runs away from the from the camera position.

Follow Shot

A follow shot in a movie is when the camera follows the action of a subject from a fixed position using tilts or pans.

Editorial shots

The next two shots are editorial shots. These types of shots are employed to assist in telling the story. The middle frame is a wide shot that establishes that the scene is taking place in a church yard. The last shot is of a gravestone and is a cutaway shot because this subject was not depicted in the establishing shot.

Establishing Shot

An establishing shot is a wide shot (WS) or a long shot (LS) that provides an audience a basic orientation to the geography of a scene.

Cutaway

A cutaway shot is a shot of part of a scene but is filmed from a different angle and/or focal length from the master shot; it portrays action not covered in the master shot.

Follow Shot

Establishing Shot

Cutaway

FIGURE 2.6-11. A storyboard showing both camera movement and editorial shots.

There are two shots on this board (Figure 2.6-12) that are both in the editorial category. The first is a match cut (or dissolve) shot. The camera is close to an eye of the gravestone from the previous board. The next frame shows the moon as a subject with a size about the same as the eye. In editing, these two frames will dissolve together.

In the last shot on this board, the camera frame is from the point of view of our subject. In this case, the werewolf is looking down at his hands.

Match Cut (Dissolve)

Match cut or match dissolve is a cut from one scene to a completely different scene, however, the objects in the two scenes occupy the same place in the frame.

Point-of-View Shot (POV)

A point-of-view shot shows what a subject is looking at through the camera perspective.

BRIEF REVIEW OF TERMS:

CUT Calling "cut" stops filming when in production. In editing, it means to make an abrupt change of image or sound, or changing from one shot to another.

DISSOLVE A transition between scenes where one fades away and the other fades in simultaneously.

EDIT The act of deleting, arranging, and placing together shots and sounds in order to construct a flowing sequence.

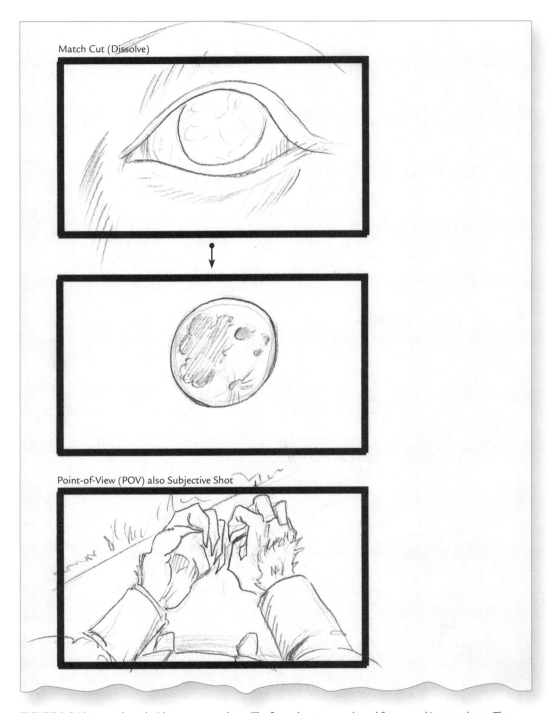

FIGURE 2.6-12. A storyboard with two camera shots. The first takes two storyboard frames and is a match cut. The second is a point-of-view shot and is also a subjective shot.

Editorial shots drive the storytelling aspect of a film's production and are used to ensure an appropriate flow to the film's sequences.

Master Shot
The master shot is the filming of an entire scene, from start to finish, and from an angle that generally keeps all the players in view.

Reaction Shot
An actor or actors are shown reacting to another actor's action or words, or to an event that is witnessed.

Objective Shot
The objective shot is not seen from the subject's point of view.

Subjective Shot
A subjective shot is taken from a subject's point of view.

Further Examples of Storyboards and Camera Shots

In Figure 2.6-13, the first frame in this storyboard is a freeze-frame shot. This type of shot is hard to depict in a storyboard frame because it is created in the postproduction phase with editing. The same is true for the jump-cut edit.

Freeze-Frame Shot
A freeze frame is a still, motionless scene or image in the course of a shot made by running a series of identical frames or by stopping at one desired frame. This shot is part of the editorial category.

Jump Cut
An edit where the middle section of a continuous shot is removed and the beginning and end of the shot are then joined together. Any moving objects in the shot will appear to jump to a new position. This shot is part of the editorial category.

Freeze-Frame Shot

Hand-Held

FIGURE 2.6-13. A storyboard with two frames. One shows a freeze-frame shot and the other hand-held shot. Only the hand-held shot frame is showing motion.

The last storyboard frame shows the camera moving with the use of arrows drawn into the frame. "Hand held" is written inside the arrow to indicate how the camera will be held for filming this shot.

Hand-Held
Hand-held is a shooting technique in which the camera is held in the operator's hands. This shot is part of the camera-movement category.

2.7 - How detailed do the storyboard drawings have to be?

Generally storyboards are drawn quickly and without elaborate detail. The goal is to clearly communicate the specifics of a shot, not to rival Michelangelo. Artistic quality is usually secondary. That is not to say that quality is unimportant, just that functionality is of primary consideration. A board that is made up of quick line drawings is just as useful as a nicely drawn and shaded board if it communicates the intended information correctly. If a board is well drawn and detailed but is unable to inform the desired shot, it fails in its use. However, keeping the overall shot concepts in mind, a more detailed board will be able to increase the amount of information being communicated. A balance between functionality and artistry is ideal.

Like graphic novels, boards depict a visual portrayal of text. Unlike comics, they are not the end product but are used as stepping stones toward depicting a moving image and might need to be created or changed quickly. Because time is a major factor, speed and accuracy is more important than elaborate artistic detail.

FIGURE 2.7. The drawing on the left is not optimally artistic, but it does show that the camera shot is a single-subject frontal close-up.

Directors sometimes draw their own storyboards to help them generate and clarify their ideas (Figure 2.7). Not all directors are artists, but even untrained line sketches can help convey their concepts. Professional storyboard artists often use those sketches as a starting point to draw more detailed and effective boards. There are also new computer programs available with predrawn figures, backgrounds, and props that enable filmmakers who might not be artistic to develop their own boards.

The following quote from Nick Noyes discusses the detail in his storyboards.

2.8 - Who benefits from storyboards and why?

The storyboarding process will benefit every department. Because the director is in charge of production, the more prepared she is, the better prepared the crew can be. It is often said that the best offense is a good defense. The same can be said for movie making and computer-game creation. A smooth production is often the result of adequate preproduction. The more thoughtfully planned out a project is in preproduction, the less potential there will be for problems during production.

Crew in preproduction

Film or game projects can be extensive, with responsibilities that are divided among various departments. Many highly trained and skilled people work on all aspects of the production at any given time, many voices with many ideas. The possibility for miscommunication is high, even on smaller crews. Given that a storyboard serves as a window for the crew to understand what the ultimate product might look like, confusion is lessened, which allows the crew to work more efficiently. All departments need a clear and concise plan in order to move forward. In some instances, it is very difficult for certain departments to accurately complete their work without a clear storyboard. This is especially true the more difficult a desired shot becomes. With the prodigious use of tools such as visual effects, it becomes far more important to be prepared in order to capture a shot as intended—on time and on budget. A clear, single voice is needed, and in many ways the storyboard will help to relay that voice. Crew members will understand the director's intentions clearly and will see them in one place.

Crew and cast during production

In addition to the players in the preproduction, additional cast and crew will find the boards helpful to have on set. The size of the cast and crew and who they are depends on the size and type of the production. The list can be very long; however, listed below are some of the main departments to represent examples of how storyboards affect every aspect of the production.

Director

Time can be a demanding aspect on set. If the shoot is running long, or if unforeseen events push the production schedule back on the time chart, the director can take a look at the storyboard and review what shots are essential and what could be cut if pressed. The storyboard makes it easier for the director to make on-set editorial cuts by removing storyboard frames or rearranging them without the deleted shots to see if the cuts will drastically affect the flow or the storytelling.

Also, there are times when the storyboards act as the shot list. The director will shoot a shot off the board and cross it off to mark the progression. Sometimes storyboards might be in binders or perhaps posted on a larger board. On other occasions, the director might ask the video technician for a review of the action that was just shot and will compare it with the storyboard. Once satisfied, a still from the shot that matches the board is printed and posted next to the storyboard. This works two fold, as a means to see the comparison, and to cross the shot off the list of what still needs to be done.

The Director of Photography

The in-production use of the storyboards by the director of photography is similar to the director's use: as a guide to the progress on each day of shooting. The storyboards are also used as a reminder of the type and style of shots that were discussed in preproduction.

Producer

Storyboards will allow the producer to check on the progress of the day's shoot and to try to keep the production running on time.

Cast (talent)

Many cast members like to visualize their performance before the cameras start shooting. Sometimes stand-ins are used for blocking and other preparations before the set is ready for the cast. The storyboards allow the cast to see where the camera is in relation to their position on the set. The cast members can track camera movement and angle changes. This allows them to have a better understanding of the set and camera frame for their mental walkthrough and can enhance their performances.

Sound

The sound-recording artist can use the storyboards to locate appropriate spots to plant their mikes to capture the desired sound. The sound recorder can also understand a little of the style of the film. This helps them when recording different ambient and wild sounds.

Gaffer (lighting)

The director and the director of photography will direct how the light should be used, but the storyboards help the gaffer understand what types of equipment might be used and if there are any special lighting techniques they can prepare for.

The following is a quote from Alex Fernbach about storyboards helping in crew meetings.

QUOTE

ALEX FERNBACH - DIRECTOR / CAMERAMAN

ARF&CO

I hold a crew meeting every day I am on set, whether it is a prep day or a shoot day, location or studio. It does not matter. This meeting is held in front of some form of storyboard. One in the order of the storyline, and next to it is the order we plan on shooting the production. Even if there was no storyboard artist, I will either take snapshots to represent the frame, or work in 3-D and output key frames to illustrate the idea.

SUMMARY

Storyboarding is a process that begins with the script, coupled with the director's interpretation of that text. The director takes notes on the script and possibly draws rough sketches or thumbnails to represent shots. The storyboard artist must gather the preproduction information such as the shot list, illustrations, diagrams, and must attend meetings with the development team or director. For the storyboard projects for video games, the artist also has other factors to be concerned with, such as user involvement and gameplay.

Aspect ratio is determined by the relationship of the height of the frame to its width. To effectively depict a scene, the storyboard artist needs to understand composition, camera placement, and angles. The artist also must become familiar with illustrating movement. A shot can be described by a variety of categories including: scale, angle, movement, and editing segues. Generally storyboards are drawn quickly and without elaborate detail. The goal is to clearly communicate the specifics of a shot. The storyboarding process benefits every department.

REVIEW QUESTIONS: CHAPTER 2

1. Where do you start a storyboard project?
2. Who should be involved?
3. What information needs to be gathered?
4. What is a shot list?
5. What are the different kinds of common types of camera shots?
6. How detailed do the storyboard drawings have to be?
7. Who benefits from storyboards and why?

1. Brainstorm a story, write a script, and plan a storyboard. If you can, work together with other people in a group.

2. Review a short movie and discuss the different camera shots, movements, or camera's point of view.

3. Develop a storyboard, showing main ideas and supporting details in a narrative, by illustrating important scenes in the story and explaining the scenes using the vocabulary in this book.

4. Keep a journal recalling the important information and thoughts from the text and write how you will use the information.

5. Write an outline about where to start making a storyboard, who's involved, information needed, and the types of shots needed.

APPLYING WHAT YOU HAVE LEARNED

1. Cut out pictures in a magazine or advertisement and label the kind of shot that was used.

2. Write the definitions of ten different common shots and draw examples of them.

3. Draw four different kinds of shots and label them.

4. Draw a quick sketch and then a second sketch incorporating more detail, using the same idea.

5. After a short story is read, draw a storyboard for one of the scenes.

6. Using the following blank storyboard frames, write a script description and identify the shot types for each frame.

Blank storyboard frames for practice

FIGURE EX-4. Practice (1.78:1 - High definition) storyboard frames for drawing.

PART 2

THE PROJECT
OVERTIME

FIGURE PO2. A storyboard frame with motion arrows.

CHAPTER 3
Preproduction

CHAPTER 4
Production

Preproduction

OVERVIEW AND LEARNING OBJECTIVES

In this chapter:

- 3.1 - Information gathering
    - a. The *Overtime* script without notation
    - b. The *Overtime* shot list
    - c. Location diagrams. Talent and location photographs
    - d. Prop and wardrobe list for the project *Overtime*
    - e. A director meeting with the storyboard artist during preproduction

- 3.2 - Refining the information
    - a. The *Overtime* script with director notation
    - b. The script to rough storyboard comparison
    - c. The shot list to storyboard comparison
    - d. Location and talent photographs to storyboard comparison
    - e. Prop and wardrobe photographs to storyboard comparison

Part one of this book covers what storyboards are and why they are an important part of filmmaking. In part two, we will walk you through the process of making storyboards on an actual project. By using the short film *Overtime* as an example, we will focus on how storyboards affect a film from preproduction to its final cut (Figure 3.1-1).

The following chapter includes information about all of the elements that need to be gathered by the storyboard artist in preproduction. Section 3.1 discusses the initial steps of translating the script into images. The script and shot list are still unmarked. The location, talent, and prop photographs and the location overhead diagrams are shown, and a mock storyboarding meeting with the director is dialogued.

The storyboard artist helps the director to clearly communicate visual ideas during preproduction. Although helpful and more polished, the storyboard drawings, the photographs, and the diagram illustrations do not have to be created on a professional level, artistically. Filmmakers can benefit from using quick stick-figure sketches and photographs to effectively communicate the desired information.

In Section 3.2 we will study the information that has been gathered and will start to refine the ideas in order to effect clear communication. We follow the translation of the script into the storyboards with the use of side-by-side storyboard comparisons as well as accompanying point-of-view commentaries.

3.1 - Information gathering

Many elements are needed to create clear and accurate storyboards. It is important to remember that the storyboard will, in essence, be the film in illustration form. The goal is for the boards to be as close a representation of the intended film image as possible. To do that, we must begin where all projects start: the script. Then, we will gather all the necessary information available from the various departments that are working in preproduction.

Let's review the list:

- Location and set diagrams
- Meetings between the director and the storyboard artist
- Prop list
- Script
- Shot list
- Talent and location photographs

Depending on the project's size and budget, this list might change; however, the basic concepts remain the same. The more comprehensive the information gathered, the more clearly the information can be communicated in preproduction, and the smoother the production phase will run.

The time line is a linear visual reference, however, it is not definitive (Figure 3.1-2). The steps might combine or run congruently depending on the size and type of the production. Overall however, the director's time line starts with reading the script, and the storyboard artist collaboration starts with meetings with the director, during which the artist will be given the shot list, diagrams, and related photographs.

The *director* is the central figure and storyteller of the film project and drives what type of information is collected or created and when it is collected or created. Although every director has their own style and methods, from the storyboard artist's perspective, the end result is similar.

The storyboard artist's job is to effectively communicate the director's vision of the story from the point of view of the camera. The artist absorbs all this information and talks with the director in order to clarify how to sketch the storyboards. The more complete and clear the information given to the artist, the more closely the storyboards will represent the final shoot.

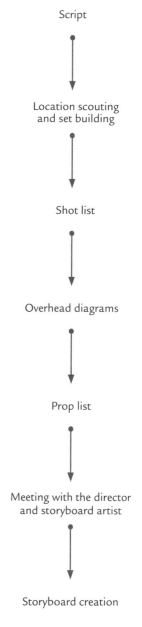

Common storyboard time line in preproduction

Script

↓

Location scouting and set building

↓

Shot list

↓

Overhead diagrams

↓

Prop list

↓

Meeting with the director and storyboard artist

↓

Storyboard creation

FIGURE 3.1-1. The film crew during the shoot of *Overtime.* An example of all of the preproduction information (props, location, cast) coming together for the shoot.

FIGURE 3.1-2. Common check list for storyboard creation.

3.1a - The *Overtime* script without notation

In the following few pages is the unmarked, original script for the project *Overtime* (Figures 3.1a-1 through 3.1a-9). A director will read a script and start to consider how to most effectively tell the story, what the style should be, and what camera movements will best represent what is going to be communicated. Some directors will draw thumbnails; others will take notes after reading the script.

This is where the storytelling procedure starts. The director will work and re-work ideas concerning the script.

- Is the story a comedy, a drama, a thriller?

- What type of cinematography will enhance the story?

- What type of soundtrack fits the stylization?

- What type of production design, wardrobe, and props?

The process of answering these questions is known as the director's *script breakdown*. From this, the shot list will emerge together with the style of the project. A number of preproduction documents will start with the script, however, in this book we have concentrated on what directly impacts the storyboard artist.

In Section 3.2a we will look at a marked-up script and read the director's commentary on how the script was broken down into scenes for the telling of the story.

BRIEF REVIEW OF TERMS:

SCRIPT BREAKDOWN A list of the basics elements of the project, including special items, equipment, and effects that are necessary for the project.

CINEMATOGRAPHY The artistic creation of moving images using light and cameras.

DIRECTOR A person who controls the creative aspects (translating the screenplay into images and sounds) of a project and instructs the cast and crew.

Overtime – v2

FADE IN:

EXT. QUIET CITY STREET – DAY

RACHEL (32) looks a bit out of place as a phone repair worker, with sunglasses and a wig but she walks around with a sense of purpose.

She hesitates at the corner, looking up at some windows above her. When she looks back down, a FAMILIAR CAR parks itself across the street. Rage passes over her face, and then she settles down and waltzes over.

> RACHEL
>
> You're blowing my cover.

MICHELE (28), a severe looking young woman, nearly jumps into the passenger's seat. Then she recognizes Rachel and recovers.

> MICHELE
>
> The wind is blowing your cover!

Rachel grabs her collar, nearly yanking her from the car.

> RACHEL
>
> I'm being nice. Scram, before I call the boss on you.

FIGURE 3.1A-1. The first page of the unmarked script.

MICHELE

On ME? Seriously, is
that the best you got!!!

MICHELE ducks for cover. A MYSTERIOUS MAN
(50) is locking the door to his apartment.

Rachel, already leaning into the car, sees
the man and DIVES INTO THE CAR. Legs and
boots get pulled in the window just as the
Man turns around.

INT. CAR - DAY

They're in pain, but too scared to move.

MICHELE

Did he see us?

RACHEL

I don't think so. Let me
check.

She pulls out a compact and lifts the little
mirror above the dash.

In the mirror, the Man gets into his car.

RACHEL

No. Thank god . . . Don't
just lie there, follow
him!

FIGURE 3.1A-2. The second page of the script.

They straighten themselves out, Michele
fighting to keep the driver's seat.

EXT. DIVE BAR - DAY

The Man pulls up in front of the old bar
across the street. Michele and Rachel watch
him go in.

                    RACHEL
          Stay here. He'll notice
          you.

                    MICHELE
          Yeah, and you're going
          to blend into the
          woodwork in that getup
          -- or you have a spare
          dress stuffed in that
          belt?

Smiling sweetly, Rachel reaches into a pocket
- DRAGGING OUT A DRESS.

EXT. DIVE BAR -- MICHELE'S CAR - SAME DAY

An ODDLY DRESSED WOMAN with short hair gets
out of Michele's car.

                    RACHEL
          You keep watch, Michele.

Rachel leaves, and Michele grabs the wig and
sunglasses Rachel left on the car seat.

FIGURE 3.1A-3. The third page of the unmarked script.

INT. DIVE BAR - SAME DAY

It's not too crowded. There are tables for
lunch, but nobody eating.

The Man is ordering some beers, so Rachel
leans against the end of the bar.

MICHELE walks in wearing Rachel's wig and
sunglasses! But she is acting tough enough to
frighten the men off.

Michele strides to the bar, standing next to
the Man -- without being recognized.

Rachel moves up from the end of the bar;
getting so close the Man bumps her.

                    MAN
            Excuse me.

No hint of him recognized Rachel. Rachel
thinks she is winning their game.

Then the Man spots Michele - instant
interest. Michele beams. Oh yeah, now Michele
winning the game!

Door chimes ring. A MYSTERIOUS WOMAN (?)
enters the bar. She's sexy, tough -- and both
women hate her.

The Man grabs his beers and runs toward the
mysterious woman, leading her to a table.

Rachel moves first, getting the closer table.
Michele settles for a table COVERED WITH
PLATES FROM THE PREVIOUS DINER.

FIGURE 3.1A-4. The fourth page of the unmarked script.

As they watch, the Man and the woman lean close. She pushes her beer aside, whispers something. The Man turns aside to grab the beer back.

                    MAN
          Scotch, please, make it
          a double.

While the man is distracted, the Woman sprinkles powder into his beer.

Both Michele and Rachel sit up, alert – but are afraid of blowing their cover!

Panicked, Michele forks a bit of food and FLINGS IT at the man. It lands in his beer!

The man looks over, and Michele acts innocent.

They go back to talking until the chicken wings arrive.

AT THE TABLE the woman talks in the Man's ear, trying to hold his gaze while her hand SPRINKLES more powder onto the chicken wings.

Then she gives Michele a cold stare while the Man picks up a chicken wing.

They're both panicked, but what to do?

Rachel grabs a bottle of ketchup.

He raises the chicken wing toward his mouth to take a bite.

FIGURE 3.1A-5. The fifth page of the unmarked script.

Rachel squirts ketchup all over the Man's
face!

Spitting, the Man wipes it off and leaps to
his feet.

                    MAN
          You want a piece of me?

                    RACHEL
          Yeah! Yeah, I – sorta
          do.

                    MAN
          Do I know you?

                    WOMAN
          Honey, let's just get
          out of here.

Michele leaps to her feet – knocking over the
small table where she was sitting.

                    MICHELE
          Illidia? Illidia Snow!

The Woman pauses nonchalantly then knocks
Michele into her seat, and heads for the
back. The Man is torn between fighting Rachel
and following his sweetheart – which allows
Michele to chase after her.

FIGURE 3.1A-6. The sixth page of the unmarked script.

EXT. DIVE BAR - SAME DAY

Michele bursts out of the door - there's
nobody there. The woman vanished.

The back door opens. Michele spins around and
Illidia catches her, and throws Michele to
the ground.

                    ILLIDIA
              Michele Estavanti, you
              stole my boyfriend.
              Prepare to die!

Illidia lifts her hand to strike. From
behind, Rachel grabs it!

Two against one - it is unfair odds. Illidia
counters Rachel's every move while knocking
Michele down every time she attempts to get
up. Illidia is having fun.

Police lights dance across the wall. They all
turn, look into the light, and find the Man
standing there.

                    MAN
              Illidia Snow, you're
              under arrest.

                    ILLIDIA
              Honey . . . lose my
              number!

FIGURE 3.1A-7. The seventh page of the unmarked script.

She throws both Rachel and Michele toward the Man and is gone before anybody can get to their feet. A plain clothes agent chases after Illidia.

                    MAN

          What are you two doing
          here?

                  MICHELE

          Rachel dared me to come
          here dressed like this.

                    MAN

          But – how did you know
          that was Illidia?

                  MICHELE

          She made high school
          living hell.

                    MAN

          Go home and stay out
          of trouble. Let the
          professionals handle
          this – Oh, and thank
          you. Good to know you
          have my back.

The Man runs off. Michele and Rachel finally relax – or just plain collapse.

FIGURE 3.1A-8. The eighth page of the unmarked script.

                    RACHEL

          We have GOT to stop
          stalking him! It isn't
          healthy.

                    MICHELE

          Are you kidding? Our
          stalking saved his life!

                    RACHEL

          HE'S the FBI agent. We're
          just office assistants.

                    MICHELE

          We're more than that.
          We're better than that!

But they aren't, and they know it.

                    MICHELE

          Hey, I bet there are
          people the FBI would pay
          us to stalk.

                    RACHEL

          Yeah. We're kind of good
          at it, aren't we?

                    MICHELE

          Yeah, we kinda are.

They punch knuckles together and head off arm
in arm.

FIGURE 3.1A-9. The ninth page of the unmarked script.

3.1b - The *Overtime* shot list unmarked

After reading the script, the director will break down how the story will be told. Part of that process is to decide how and where the camera should be used to effectively tell the story.

The following pages include the original *shot list* for the project *Overtime* (Figures 3.1b-1 through 3.1b-3). The director broke down the script into six scenes. Within the six different scenes there are a number of shots with a variety of camera positions, angles, and movements. The shot list is the written road map to the shoot; the storyboards are the visual map.

In Section 2.6, some common types of shots were illustrated with accompanying definitions. It is important that the storyboard artist recognize and understand the terminology and the abbreviations in the shot list.

The scenes start with a master shot followed by close-ups, cutaways, and camera movement directions for complete *coverage*. The grayed-out lines are indicators that a shot can be cut for time or budgetary matters. In scene three, the grayed shot D: *MCU – SNAP ZOOM* (Figure 3.1b-1, Bottom) was cut from filming, and Rachel's reveal of her dress under her overalls was covered in an over-the-shoulder shot.

The shot list, together with the overhead diagrams, help to create film documents such as a *shooting schedule,* as well as the storyboards.

BRIEF REVIEW OF TERMS:

COVERAGE Shooting a scene from many different angles in order to properly tell the story.

SHOOTING SCHEDULE A projected plan of each day's shooting for a production.

SHOT LIST A form constructed to show all intended shots in a production.

MEDIUM CLOSE-UP (MCU) A shot that is cropped between the shoulders and the chest.

Overtime

SHOT LIST

SC#1 — Scene Heading

A- MS- City Street, Camera **GLIDES** tilted toward the ground revealing high heels in full stride. We tilt up to reveal Rachel wearing overalls and carry a utility bag. We swing OTS and continue to track with her capturing her rhythmic step. She trips. (MASTER)–Rachel settles at the corner and ruffles through her utility bag. She looks up at window checks her watch then spots a familiar car pulling up. Rachel turns away then walks to the car, talks to Michele and jumps in as the Man exits building. Car follows Man.

A1 MCU- Rachel's Face as she walks.

Shot Heading

B- MS (OTS)- Rachel pops down into driver's side window, scares Michele.

C- MS (OTS)- Michele.

D- FS- Man (from inside car)

SC#2 — Type of Shot

A- 2SHOT *(dutch)*- Rachel and Michele scrunched in car.

B- CU Mirror (HH)- CAM pushing in.

C- 2SHOT (Pass window)- Rachel and Michele untangle themselves, pop up & drive off.

SC#3

A- WS (*low angle*)- EXT BAR, CAM **GLIDES** off a parked car as the Man's car pulls into lot. Michele's car pulls in and lingers behind.

A1-2 SHOT- Rachel and Michele in car.

B- 2SHOT (behind car)- Rachel and Michele watch the Man enter the bar.

C- INSERT – Man entering Bar.

D- MCU – **SNAP ZOOM** as Rachel reveals clothes.

FIGURE 3.1B-1. The first page of the shot list, including scenes one through three.

SC#4 – EXT BAR – MOMENTS LATER

A- FS (*slo mo*)- CAM, low angle, **SLIDES** in as Rachel exits car.

B- MS (OTS)- Rachel drops into pass window. Tilt down to reveal wig and glasses.

C- CU- Wig and glasses.

SC#5 – INT BAR- DAY

A- WS (MASTER)- Rachel walks up to bar as the Man orders a drink at bar. Michele enters and walks to the bar. Rachel moves closer and bumps man. Woman enters everyone sits.

B- CU- beer slams on bar counter.

C- MS (*slo mo*)- Michele enters bar.

D- 3 SHOT- Rachel notices Michele enter. Michele takes position next to Man. Cover to when Michele sits at table.

E- MS- CAM **SLIDES** as Ilidia enters bar and meets with Man. He leads her to table.

F- WS- Man moves to table with Ilidia.

G- 2 SHOT- Man and Ilidia sit.

H- CU- Ilidia at table. Tilt to reveal her powdering wings.

I- CU- Ilidia puts powder in Man's drink.

J- CU – Rachel

K- CU- Michele

L- CU- Man at table

Shot that could be cut

M- WS- They stand. Ilidia knocks Michele over and exits.

FIGURE 3.1B-2. The second page of the shot list, including scenes four and five.

SC#6 – EXT BAR – CONTINUOUS

A- FS (MASTER)- CAM *GLIDES* in as Michele storms out of the bar. Swing around to behind Michele to reveal Ilidia gone. Ilidia steps into frame and fight ensues with Rachel entering. The Man comes and Illidia escapes. Rachel and Michele are victorious.

B- WS- Fight - Illidia throws Rachel and Michele at Man and escapes. Man says thanks.

C- CU- Michele on ground.

D- CU- Illidia- Tilt up to Illidia's hand as she's about to strike. Rachel grabs Illidia.

E- MCU- Fight, float between Rachel & Michele

F- FS- Man

G- 3SHOT- Rachel, Man and Michele. Cover through end of scene.

H- CU- Michele

I- CU- Rachel

This blank area respresents the end of the shot list and the end of the film.

FIGURE 3.1B-3. The last page of the shot list, including scene six. The final scene.

3.1c - Location diagrams. Talent and location photographs

Scouting for a *location* and building a set are art forms in themselves. They are the visual environment for the story. Production designers and their staffs try to build or find the perfect setting in which to envelop the viewer with the director's story. The importance of the location photographs and diagrams should not be overlooked.

The two-day shoot for project *Overtime* took place in both an inside and an outside location. We scouted a few locations and selected Morin's Diner. Photographs and quick sketches were made. The images helped the director plan the two-day shoot and the storyboard artist to accurately represent the location in the drawings. The location sketches were later developed into overhead diagrams (Figure 3.1c-1).

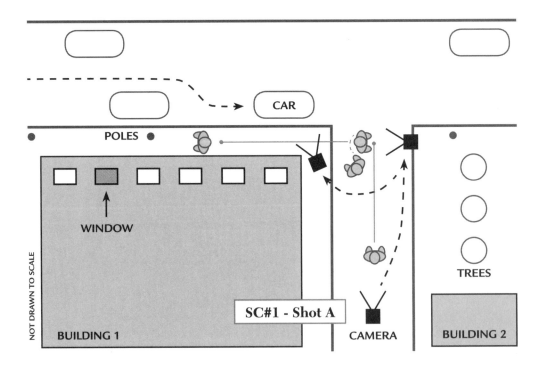

FIGURE 3.1C-1. This diagram is of the outside street area. In the final shoot, the movement of the car was changed to park on the left side of the road, for safety reasons

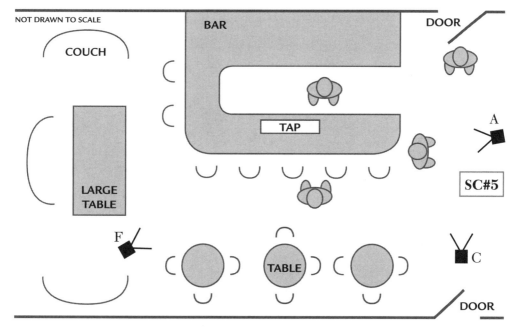

FIGURE 3.1C-2. This diagram is of the inside bar area. It is an early draft for the camera placement. Even if the diagram is a quick sketch on a scrap piece of paper, thinking about the camera positioning will help your production.

Location diagrams

Overhead location diagrams are used to illustrate camera placement within a set or location for particular shots. They are a great tool used not only by the storyboard artist but also by directors, assistant directors, and directors of photography. Storyboard artists use the diagrams to supplement location photographs and to clarify exactly where a camera *setup* will be. By looking at the diagram, the artist can estimate what the camera will pick up behind the actor, making certain the shot is captured accurately in the drawings. Utilizing tools such as this helps professional storyboard artists execute their drawings with precision (Figure 3.1c-2).

> **BRIEF REVIEW OF TERMS:**
>
> **LOCATION / FILMING LOCATION** The place where some or all of a project is produced, in addition to or instead of using constructed sets.
>
> **SET** The location where shooting is taking place, either indoors or outdoors.
>
> **SETUP** Each new camera angle, especially when lighting must be moved.

Location photographs

Photographs of locations and sets play a number of different, valuable roles in preproduction, including that of being a reference for artists creating the diagrams and storyboards (Figure 3.1c-3).

FIGURE 3.1C-3. Two location photographs from inside the bar.

Talent photographs

Images of the cast are always used when made available to the storyboard artist. Actor headshots are often the reference of choice for drawing talent likenesses. For this book, we used stills from the short film *Overtime* as examples (Figure 3.1c-4).

FIGURE 3.1C-4. From the upper left Rachel - Ramona Taj; upper right Michele Estavanti - Leighsa Burgin; lower left, Illidia Snow - Alisha Finneran; lower right, FBI Agent - Fiore Leo.

3.1d - Prop and wardrobe list for the project *Overtime*

Although it may not be as important for this short film as it might be in other films, it is always a good practice to check if any props or wardrobe pieces are unique. Images or descriptions of these items will help the storyboards to closely depict how the objects will look when filmed (Figure 3.1d).

FIGURE 3.1D. A sampling of props from *Overtime*. Left - Rachel's dress; top right - phone equipment; lower right - compact mirror.

Original prop list

- Phone repair equipment
- Overalls for phone worker
- Wig, sunglasses, gum
- Old car with one large front bench-style seat
- Chicken wings
- Table food
- Beers (nonalcoholic)
- Scotch (apple juice)
- Two white-button dress shirts
- Squeeze bottle ketchup
- Powder and a bag for the powder
- Police light
- Undercover car
- Dress and high heels
- Beer and scotch glasses
- Compact mirror

3.1e - A director meeting with the storyboard artist during preproduction

The importance of meeting with the director during preproduction was discussed in Section 2.2 and 2.3. In this chapter, we have created an outline example of a meeting for the project *Overtime*. To review, the number of members at the meeting will vary; usually only the storyboard artist and the director will meet, but occasionally the director of photography, production designer, or producer could be present as well.

The director provides the overall vision and storytelling style of the project, while the director of photography, who will be executing the shots, will provide insight regarding camera techniques. The production designer will help execute the director's vision through set design and art direction, and the producer will usually manage the ideas from a logistical and budgetary point of view. The storyboard artist will take notes based on the director's vision and the shot list. Sometimes the artist quickly sketches the ideas so that everyone in the meeting can see them come to life. This also helps everyone to determine what will be effective and what will not (Figure 3.1e).

A preproduction meeting dialogue

The next few pages represent a fictional dialogue that could transpire during a preproduction meeting. The text is slightly different than the actual meeting dialogue for *Overtime*. The dialogue changes were made to represent the points of view of the meeting attendants should they all be present during the meeting at once. The speakers in the dialogue are indicated by their titles.

Director: Thanks for coming everyone. I wanted to review the opening shot sequence of the film. I thought a lot about how the story should start and wanted to talk about how I'd like to execute it.

My visual strategy for the film is sort of "old Bond meets new Bourne" while, of course maintaining a comedic edge to it. I envision starting with smoother camera moves, then transitioning to hand-held camera for the end.

Let's take it from the top, scene 1, shot A on the shot list. We start with a *MCU*. I want to reveal character in the opening shot. I'd like to have Rachel wearing high heels with her undercover telephone overalls. That will tell something of her and have some comedic value. For the camera reveal I want to move with her, using one long shot that starts low and close to the street, then tilts up to the heels and then Rachel's overalls. The camera will then move around to the front of her.

Producer: I am sorry, but we do not have the budget for a steadicam. We have some for wardrobe and props, but not enough for extra camera equipment.

Director of Photography: I have a camera stabilizer that might work for the shot you are thinking of. It is a hand-held stabilizer that was built by hand, but it should work.

Director: It might. It would be better than the camera being just hand held and if we don't have the budget to rent a steadicam then we can test it out and see how it works.

Director of Photography: How long of a move were you looking for?

Director: We should carry Rachel all the way until the story introduces Michele for the first time. The shot will be long, but dynamic if we get the timing right. Do we have an overhead diagram of our location?

Director of Photography: And any location photographs? I'd like to see how much space we have for the move.

Production Designer: Yes, here they are.

Director: Take a look, if we start on this side of the alley, have Rachel walk toward the street and park the car just to the left of the alley opening, it should be able to be shot all in one continuous shot.

Storyboard Artist: Ok, I see now. We start low, tilt up as she's walking, circle the camera around Rachel, then pan back toward the street as the car pulls up. Do you want to be in MCU the whole time?

Director: I do at first. In the opening I want the audience to see the high heels and maybe expect to see a dress when the camera tilts up to reveal the undercover overalls. But as she turns away from camera to go to the car, we'll let the frame stay wide and drift toward the car.

Production Designer: Do you ever plan on looking back away from the building toward the other end of the street? If so, I'll need to come up with a way to dress that area.

Director: No, don't worry about over there. We'll frame that out.

Storyboard Artist: I've got a question before I start to sketch. You said a moving shot starting from the heels then tilting up. Did you want to be directly behind the heels or from either three-quarters to the left or right?

Director: I want to be directly behind the heels as we tilt up.

Storyboard Artist: Can I see the location photographs? When the script calls for Rachel to look up at some windows, which one is she looking up at?

Director: This one here. See if you can draw focus to it in your board when you sketch it out.

Storyboard Artist: How did you want to handle the camera move around Rachel; up to the window, then down to the car? Did you want a 360 degree movement around Rachel?

Director: No, I want the camera to move up after Rachel is revealed and then stop momentarily over her right shoulder. That way, we'll catch both the window and the car pulling up. Then, after Rachel sees the car, have her turn toward the camera to reveal her reaction before continuing the move.

Storyboard Artist: So, Rachel reacts toward the camera after seeing Michele's car pull up, then you want me to follow her until she reaches the car, and then pan to Michele sitting in the car?

Director: Yes, I was thinking of ending the shot with a medium shot of Michele.

Production Designer: Here, I also have pictures of Rachel's props and wardrobe for you to reference.

Producer: I have the actor's headshot with me, too. Here you go.

Storyboard Artist: To recap, you want a long tracking shot to open the film starting in MCU looking at the pavement and then titling up to high heels. After that you want the shot to move the camera to the right of Rachel. Then stop in place momentarily and tilt up when Rachel looks up at the windows. The camera then follows Rachel when she starts walking again and then drifts into Michele in the car for the final movement. Is that right?

Director: Yes, that sounds about right. Let's draw up some thumbnail sketches to make sure!

FIGURE 3.1E. These images are frames taken from the opening storyboards, with the arrows showing the camera movements. During the meetings, storyboard artists can draw brainstorming concepts so that the director can see what ideas work and what needs to be reworked.

3.2 - Refining the information

In the previous section, we explained that translating the script into shots begins with the director's first reading of the script and continues through the information-gathering phase. In this section, we will refine the breakdown into complete storyboards.

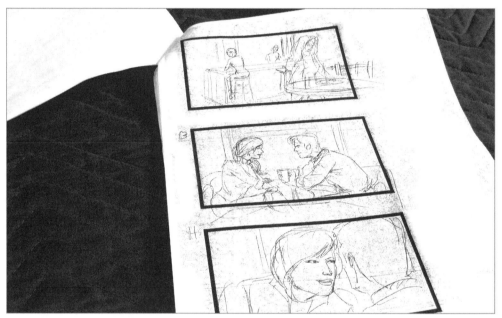

FIGURE 3.2. This is a photograph of the quick first drafts of the storyboards, used to tweak shot ideas and the flow of the story.

This script, shot list, and photographs are now marked and compared to the quick first drafts of the storyboards (Figure 3.2). With these drafts the director can begin to see what shot ideas and storytelling choices work as intended for *principal photography.* The storyboards enable the director to tweak shots before they are on set.

Once the storyboards are approved, the shift from sketching phase to completion phase will begin.

NOTE

Storyboards are sometimes used in postproduction. Their main function is for the editor to discern how the director intended to cut a scene. Because changes often take place during shooting, however, editors generally focus on what was actually shot.

In Section 3.2e all the elements come together. Each page of the storyboards for the short film is shown with the corresponding text of the script. We begin at the top of the script and continue to the final sketching of the storyboards for the complete arc from the script, to *preproduction*, and then *production*.

> **BRIEF REVIEW OF TERMS:**
>
> **POSTPRODUCTION** The general term for all stages of production occurring after the actual shooting and ending with the completed work.
>
> **PREPRODUCTION** The process of preparing all the elements involved in a project before actual shooting.
>
> **PRINCIPAL PHOTOGRAPHY** The primary phase of production in which the project is actually shot, as distinct from preproduction, postproduction, or reshoots.
>
> **PRODUCTION** The process of actual shooting of all the elements for a film project.

3.2a - The *Overtime* script with director notation

The director's interpretation of the script begins the project. The decisions the director makes dictate how materials, such as the shot list, are made.

The following script of *Overtime* is marked with notes the director made when reading the script (Figures 3.2a-1 through 3.2a-6). The marks indicate thoughts on style, beginning and ending of shots and scenes, and camera movements.

Commentary

The Director
Marking a script is simply the process of writing notes, or ideas that you intend to use for filming. The way a script is marked will depend on the preference of the director. This particular script has notes I made to myself regarding style choices, camera movements, shot numbers, and actors' blocking. I also "lined" the script to indicate how long I intended to take a particular shot throughout a scene.

Working Overtime – v2

> The number and letter represent the different scenes and shots.

FADE IN:

EXT. QUIET CITY STREET – DAY

START THE SCENE BY FOCUSING ON THE HEELS, THEN REVEAL RACHEL'S
OUTLANDISH DISGUISE.
RACHEL (24) looks a bit out of place as a phone repair worker,
FAST PACED
THE OPENING with sunglasses and a wig and heels, but she walks around with a
SHOT WILL sense of purpose. HAVE RACHEL TRIP OUT OF FRAME TO CONVEY HER
SET UP THE CLUMSY CHARACTER THEN QUICKLY POP BACK IN (BIRD LIKE)
TONE OF She hesitates at the corner, looking up at some windows above
THE FILM. her. When she looks back down a FAMILIAR CAR parks itself across
the street. Rage passes over her face, and then she settles down
and waltzes over.

MOVING CAMERA & FAST CUTS TO GIVE A SENSE
OF ENERGY & PURPOSE TO R. RACHEL
CARRY THIS ENERGY THRU OUT FILM, You're going to blow my cover.
BUT TRANSITION FROM SMOOTH CAM.
TO ROUGH CAM.
MICHELE (28), a severe looking young woman, nearly jumps into
THE IDEA the passenger's seat. Then she recognizes Rachel and recovers.
IS TO MERGE THE PREDOMINATE
STYLES OF MOST SPY MOVIES. MICHELE
SMOOTH, CONTROLLED CAM. & A stiff breeze would do that!
ROUGH HAND HELD. (OLD BOND VS. BOURNE)
Rachel grabs her collar, nearly yanking her from the car.

RACHEL
KEEP THE I'm being nice. Scram, before I
BANTER FAST call the boss on you.
PACED

MICHELE
You're going to turn me in?
Seriously, is that the best you got!!!

MICHELE ducks for cover. A MYSTERIOUS MAN (50) is locking the
door to his apartment.

Rachel, already leaning into the car, sees the man and DIVES
INTO THE CAR. Legs and boots get pulled in the
window just as the Man turns around. COMPLETE RACHEL'S JUMP
WITH CUTS TO QUICKEN SCREEN TIME & PLAY UP THE HUMOR.
INT. CAR – DAY

They're in pain, but too scared to move.
2A
(FROM REHEARSAL) RACHEL LANDS ON TOP OF
MICHELE. HAVE RACHEL ROLL OVER ON TOP OF MICHELE.
PLAY UP THEIR RELATIONSHIP W/ THIS VISUAL IMAGE
RACHEL IS ALWAYS ACCIDENTALLY AHEAD OF MICHELE

1A

1C 1B

1D

FIGURE 3.2A-1. The first page of the marked up script.

THE HIGH ANGLE, LOOKING DOWN, WILL ACCENTUATE THE ACTION &
THEIR RELATIONSHIP: COMPACT, RACHEL, MICHELE.

ALLOW THE ANGLE TO PLAY THROUGH THE ACTION. IT PLAYS FUNNY TO   2A
SEE RACHEL LAYING ON MICHELE
WHILE SPYING ON THE AGENT.

                    MICHELE
              Did he see us?

                    RACHEL
              I don't think so. Let me check.   2B

She pulls out a compact and lifts the little mirror above the
dash.

In the mirror, the Man gets into his car.

> The lines represent
> the different shots

                    RACHEL
              No. Thank god . . .

              (Smacks Michele)Don't just lie   1B
                    there, follow him!

They straighten themselves out, Michele fighting to keep the
driver's seat. FAST MOTION FROM BOTH R & M. AS THEY
           POP INTO FRAME.   WIPE OUT OF
EXT. DIVE BAR - DAY   SCENE.   3A

The Man pulls up in front of the old bar across the street. 3D 3B
Michele and Rachel watch him go in. P.O.V. SHOT FOR VOYEURISTIC 3C
                                         FEEL.

                    RACHEL
              Stay here. He'll recognize you.

                    MICHELE
              Yeah, sure, you go on – they're
              going to eat you up dressed like that!
              Or what, do you have a spare dress
              stuffed up those fake clothes of yours.

Remembering her outfit, Rachel sighs and reaches down her work
belt - DRAGGING OUT A DRESS. SNAP ZOOM INTO R. AS SHE
                REVEALS DRESS. USE THAT MOTION
EXT. DIVE BAR -- MICHELE'S CAR - SAME DAY
                     TO TRANSITION TO NEXT SCENE.
                                                                4A
An ODDLY DRESSED WOMAN with short hair gets out of Michele's
car. SHOOT THIS W/ LOW ANGLE IN SLO-MO TO REVEAL   4B
     R. IN NEW DESGUISE.
                    RACHEL
              You keep watch, Michele.

Rachel leaves, and Michele grabs the wig and sunglasses Rachel 4C

HAVE M. LOOK @ THE WIG & GLASSES THEN DELIVER A
DEVIOUS LOOK.

FIGURE 3.2A-2. The second page of the marked up script.

left on the car seat.

INT. DIVE BAR - SAME DAY   *5A*

It's not too crowded. There are tables for lunch, but nobody
eating.

The Man is ordering some beers, so Rachel leans against the end   *5D* *5B*
of the bar. RACHEL ENTERS TURNS AWAY FROM AGENT &
BACKS INTO HIM SO HE CAN'T SEE HER FACE   *5C*
MICHELE walks in wearing Rachel's wig and sunglasses! But she is
acting tough enough to frighten the men off. M. ENTERS SLO-MO
IN   IN LOW ANGLE.

Michele strides to the bar, standing next to the Man -- without
being recognized.

Rachel moves up from the end of the bar; getting so close the
Man bumps her.

                          MAN
                    Excuse me.

No hint of him recognized Rachel. Rachel thinks she is winning
their game.

Then the Man spots Michele - instant interest. Michele beams. Oh
yeah, now Michele winning the game!   *5E*

Door chimes ring. A MYSTERIOUS WOMAN (?) enters the bar. She's
sexy, tough -- and both women hate her. CAM SHOULD TRACK
              W/ I. W/ OTHERS IN FORGROUND).   *5F*
The Man grabs his beers and runs toward the mysterious woman,
leading her to a table.

Rachel moves first, getting the closer table. Michele settles
for a table COVERED WITH PLATES FROM THE PREVIOUS DINER.
                  5O *5M*   *5K* *5J*   *5H*
As they watch, the Man and the woman lean close. She pushes her
beer aside, whispers something. The Man turns aside to grab the *5G*
bar back.

                          MAN
                    Scotch, please, make it a double. *5I*

While the man is distracted, the Woman sprinkles powder into his

THE END OF THIS SCENE SHOULD BUILD
INTO A SERIES OF CROSS CUTS TO INCREASE
TENSION. M. & R SHOULD BE FRENETIC AGAINST THE INTIMACY OF
THE AGENT & ILLIDIA.

Notes for the end
of the scene.

FIGURE 3.2A-3. The third page of the marked up script.

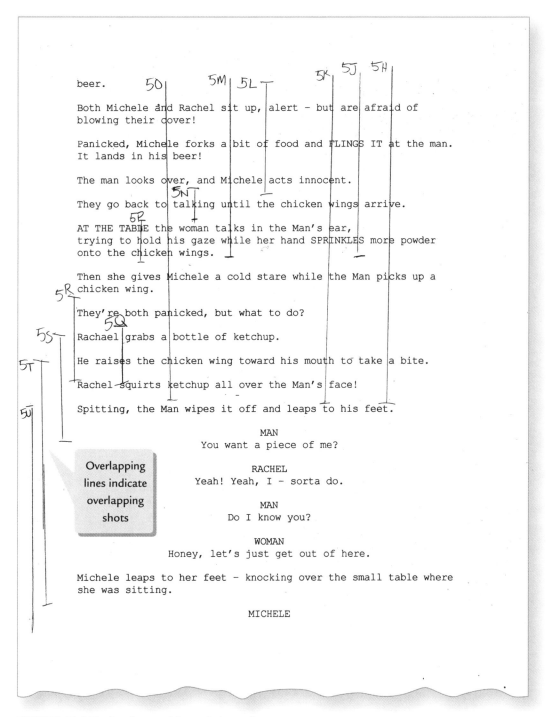

beer. 5O 5M 5L 5K 5J 5H

Both Michele and Rachel sit up, alert – but are afraid of blowing their cover!

Panicked, Michele forks a bit of food and FLINGS IT at the man. It lands in his beer!

The man looks over, and Michele acts innocent.

5N

They go back to talking until the chicken wings arrive.

5P

AT THE TABLE the woman talks in the Man's ear, trying to hold his gaze while her hand SPRINKLES more powder onto the chicken wings.

Then she gives Michele a cold stare while the Man picks up a
5R chicken wing.

They're both panicked, but what to do?

5Q

5S Rachael grabs a bottle of ketchup.

5T He raises the chicken wing toward his mouth to take a bite.

Rachel squirts ketchup all over the Man's face!

5U Spitting, the Man wipes it off and leaps to his feet.

                        MAN
            You want a piece of me?

                      RACHEL
            Yeah! Yeah, I – sorta do.

Overlapping   MAN
lines indicate   Do I know you?
overlapping
shots   WOMAN
            Honey, let's just get out of here.

Michele leaps to her feet – knocking over the small table where she was sitting.

                      MICHELE

FIGURE 3.2A-4. The fourth page of the marked up script.

Illidia? Illidia Snow?

**The Woman pauses nonchalantly then knocks Michele into her
seat, and heads for the back. The Man is torn between
fighting Rachel and following his sweetheart - which allows
Michele to chase after her.**

EXT. DIVE BAR - SAME DAY

THE FIGHT SCENE SHOULD BE SHOT HAND HELD. HIGH ENERGY!

Michele bursts out of the door - there's nobody there. The woman
vanished. *THIS FRANTIC ENERGY WILL HELP FINALIZE THE
FILMS TRANSITION FROM SMOOTH CAMERA MOVES TO ROUGH.*
The back door opens. Michele spins around and Illidia catches
her, and throws Michele to the ground.

                    ILLIDIA
          Michele Estavanti, you stole my
             boyfriend. Prepare to die!

Illidia lifts her hand to strike. From behind, Rachael grabs it!

Two against one - it is unfair odds. Illidia counters Rachael's
every move while knocking Michele down every time she attempts
to get up. Illidia is having fun.
*INCLUDE JIU JITSU IN THE FIGHT AS OPPOSED TO JUST
STRIKING TO KEEP THE ACTION INTERESTING & MODERN.*
Police lights dance across the wall. They all turn, look into
the light, and find the Man standing there.

                    MAN   *GET COMICAL
          Illidia Snow, you're under arrest.   REACTION SHOTS of
                                               R. & M. BEING BEATEN*

                    ILLIDIA
          Can't we just be friends?

She throws both Rachel and Michele toward the Man and is gone
before anybody can get to their feet. **A plain clothes agent
chases after Illidia.**

                    MAN
          What are you two doing here?

                    MICHELE
          Rachel dared me to come here dressed
                 like this.   *R- "I HAVE MAN LOVE FOR
                                          YOU."*
                    MAN

FIGURE 3.2A-5. The fifth page of the marked up script.

But — how did you know that was
Illidia?

MICHELE
She made high school living hell.

MAN
Go home and stay out of trouble.
Let the professionals handle this —
Oh, and thank you. Good to know you
have my back.

The Man runs off. Michele and Rachel finally relax — or just
plain collapse.

SLOW THE ENERGY DOWN & ALLOW THE RELATIONSHIP PLAY OUT THROUGH THE PERFORMANCES.

RACHEL
We have GOT to stop stalking him!
It isn't healthy.

MICHELE
Are you kidding? Our stalking saved
his life!

RACHEL
HE'S the FBI agent. We're just
office assistants.

MICHELE
We're more than that. We're better
than that!

But they aren't, and they know it.

MICHELE
Hey, I bet there are people the FBI
would pay us to stalk.

RACHEL
Yeah. We're kind of good at it,
aren't we?

MICHELE
Yeah, we kinda are.

They punch knuckles together and head off arm in arm.

FIGURE 3.2A-6. The sixth page of the marked up script.

3.2b - The script to rough storyboard comparison

In the next few pages, we are going to look at side-by-side comparisons of a script to the first storyboard sketches (Figures 3.2b-3 – 3.2b30). These drawings were the first indications for the director to see if the story and the types of camera shots would work as intended.

As an artist, do not spend time on shading the detail on the quick sketches. Wait until the director is final with the storyboards before adding detail and shading. Chances are, there will be many rounds of changes and corrections to the sketches that need to be worked out before the director is satisfied.

For the artist, these boards are the culmination of all the acquired information and the ideas discussed in the meetings with the director. Because storyboards are used as tools to communicate, the storyboard artist and the director have to make sure they understand each other.

Oftentimes, cast members study the storyboards to visualize their performances before they go on set. The storyboards allow the actors to see where

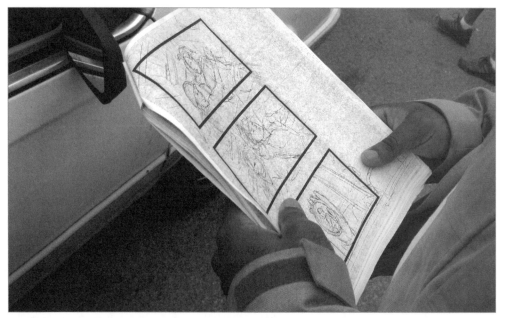

FIGURE 3.2B-1. On set, the director cannot be everywhere at once. The storyboards help communicate the director's vision to other members of the cast and crew, even when the director is busy with other tasks.

the camera will be in relation to their own positions, and they can track the camera movements. This allows them to understand what will be unfolding in the camera frame and can help them with their performances.

The storyboards might go through a number of revisions before the storyboard artist can truly depict on paper what the director is thinking. This is the last major step for the storyboards in preproduction. The clearer the storyboards are that are created in preproduction, the more clearly the information is communicated to the cast and crew in production (Figures 3.2b-1 and 3.2b-2).

Always try to have backup plans. Something will always change. The more planning you can do in preproduction phase, the smoother the production phase will be—even if complications develop.

In the following script-to-storyboard comparison, we will share both the director's thoughts and the storyboard artist's view, as well as comments by the producer, under the commentary headings.

FIGURE 3.2B-2. Cast members between takes, looking at the storyboards during production. This is an example of the cascading effect storyboards have in the production stage of the project.

```
FFADE IN:

EXT. QUIET CITY STREET - DAY

RACHEL (32) looks a bit out of place as a
phone repair worker, with sunglasses and a
wig, but she walks around with a sense of
purpose.
```

Compare the lines of text from the script to the storyboard sketch in Figure 3.2b-3.

Commentary

The Director

I wanted to open the film with energy and movement to establish the pace of the film, while using my shots to reveal character. So, I chose to start with a *tracking shot* that tilts up from the ground, revealing Rachel's heels first so that the audience is drawn in by that detail—expecting perhaps to see a dress as we continue to tilt, but instead of seeing a dress, we reveal her utility overalls. My hope is that the audience will begin to learn about Rachel's character through that camera reveal.

The Producer

We scouted a few locations before picking Morin's Diner. With this location we were able to set up for all our different types of shot sequences, including our *"Quiet City Street."* The storyboard artist received location photographs and started to sketch the opening shot. This script did not include details on how we would be introduced to Rachel or what the quiet street actually looked like, so the director's storytelling and location photographs determined these details for the storyboard artist.

BRIEF REVIEW OF TERMS:

TRACKING SHOT - A tracking shot is when the camera is being moved by means of wheels, like on a dolly.

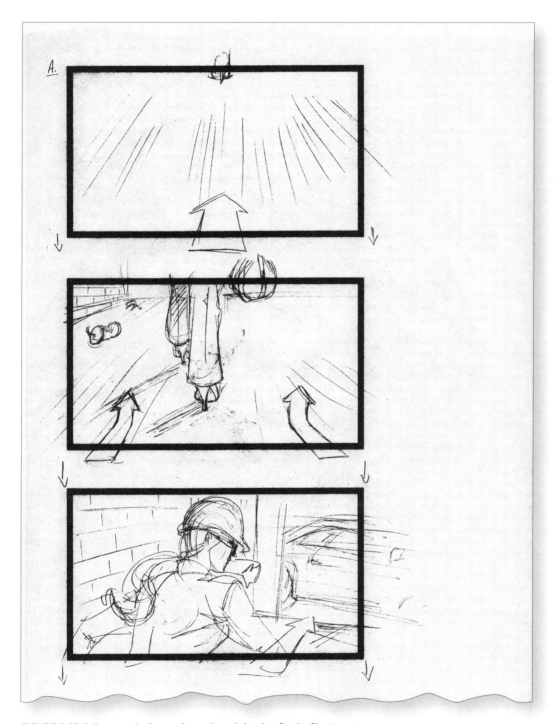

FIGURE 3.2B-3. Page one in the rough storyboard sketches for the film *Overtime*.

In Figure 3.2b-4 the storyboard continues the establishing shot and there are no corresponding lines of text in the script, but there is a description in the shot list.

As taken from the shot list:
A- MS- City Street, Camera GLIDES tilted toward the ground revealing high heels in full stride. We tilt up to reveal Rachel wearing overalls and carrying a utility bag. We swing OTS and continue to track with her, capturing her rhythmic step. She trips. (MASTER)–Rachel settles at the corner and ruffles through her utility bag. She looks up at the window, checks her watch, and then spots a familiar car pulling up. Rachel turns away and then walks to the car. She talks to Michele and jumps into the car as the Man exits building. The car follows the Man.

Commentary

The Storyboard Artist
For the opening shot, I chose to use a series of frames to illustrate the path and length of the camera move.

The Producer
The script did not go into some details, like whether Rachel was wearing high heels, whether the wall was on her left, or the camera angles tilting up and moving around Rachel. These details were all worked out by the director and brought to the page by the storyboard artist.

FIGURE 3.2B-4. Page two in the rough storyboard sketches for the film *Overtime*.

```
She hesitates at the corner, looking up at
some windows above her. When she looks back
down, a FAMILIAR CAR parks itself across the
street.
```

Compare the lines of text from the script to the storyboard sketch in Figure 3.2b-5.

Commentary

The Director
The overall visual plan for the film was to subtly marry elements from older spy films with elements from new spy films; "Old Bond meets new Bourne." I aimed to achieve this by using pans and wipes along with hand-held camera work and fast cutting.

The Storyboard Artist
As a storyboard artist, I try to capture as much of the director's intention as possible. All of the camera movement the director wanted is indicated with successive frames and arrows to indicate the direction of the camera movement. Most intentions can be captured but sometimes there are elements that will only really be evident in motion on screen. The goal is to get as close to the intention as possible

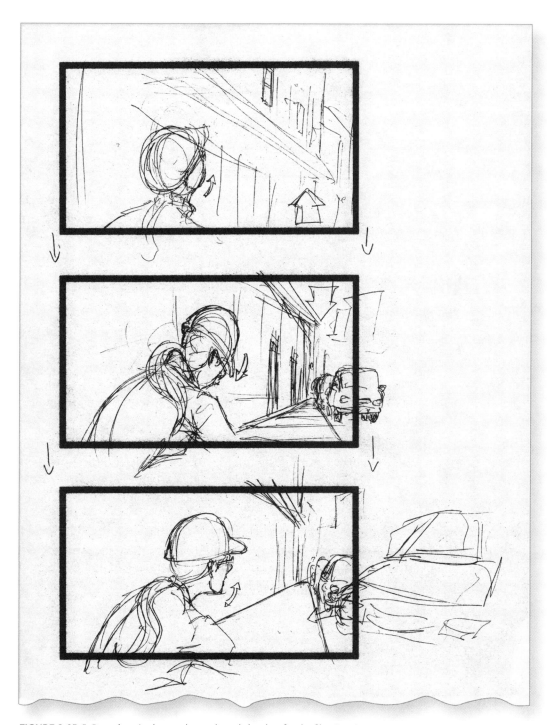

FIGURE 3.2B-5. Page three in the rough storyboard sketches for the film *Overtime.*

```
Rage passes over her face, and then she
settles down and waltzes over.
```

Compare the line of text from the script to the storyboard sketch in Figure 3.2b-6.

Commentary

The Director
I chose two camera strategies to help reveal the character traits of our two heroines:

1. I saw Rachel as being very high energy and slightly absurd. I thought of her as being bird-like, so, I used camera movement and dramatic angles on her.

2. With Michele, I wanted to be more reserved since she is the serious "straight-woman" of the film, so, in general, I tried to keep the camera more static on her, and boarded her a little more traditionally within the framework of a quickly paced and dynamic film.

The Storyboard Artist
The boards reflect the shooting strategy. The camera angles and movement were tested in the boarding phase.

FIGURE 3.2B-6. Page four in the rough storyboard sketches for the film *Overtime*.

                              RACHEL

                  You're blowing my cover.

      MICHELE (28), a severe looking young woman,
      nearly jumps into the passenger's seat. Then
      she recognizes Rachel and recovers.

                             MICHELE

                  The wind is blowing your
                  cover!

Compare the lines of text from the script to the storyboard sketch in Figure 3.2b-7.

Commentary

The Producer

For this sequence, we originally planned on having Rachel stand on the street side, but safety reasons dictated that she needed to be on the sidewalk side instead. This changed the storyboard from the original sketch.

FIGURE 3.2B-7. Page five in the rough storyboard sketches for the film *Overtime.*

```
Rachel grabs her collar, nearly yanking her
from the car.


                    RACHEL

          I'm being nice. Scram,
          before I call the boss
          on you.


                    MICHELE

          On ME? Seriously, is
          that the best you got!!!
```

Compare the lines of text from the script to the storyboard sketch in Figure 3.2b-8.

Commentary

The Director
The moment that Rachel and Michele see the agent demonstrates the shooting strategy for the characters. When Michele sees the agent, she dives down onto the seat. We boarded it so the camera does not move until Rachel jumps into the car. At that point, the camera pulls back.

The Storyboard Artist
Capturing motion in a single frame can sometimes be tricky. Aside from using arrows, one method often used is to draw the subject in motion several times along their line of travel. Usually the transitional positions are drawn lightly and the final position is drawn boldly. This helps to distinguish the movement from the final point of travel. I will most likely use this method to indicate Rachel jumping through the car window.

FIGURE 3.2B-8. Page six in the rough storyboard sketches for the film *Overtime*.

```
MICHELE ducks for cover. A MYSTERIOUS MAN
(50) is locking the door to his apartment.

Rachel, already leaning into the car, sees
the man and DIVES INTO THE CAR. Legs and
boots get pulled in the window just as the
Man turns around.
```

Compare the lines of text from the script to the storyboard sketch in Figure 3.2b-9.

Commentary

The Storyboard Artist

You will notice throughout the boards that oftentimes I will draw outside the frame lines of the shot. In general I have found that it is good practice to do this to give a sense of what is just outside the frame. Sometimes directors will look at a board and change their mind on the sizing, based on what they see in the periphery of the frame. Sometimes it is necessary to draw outside the frame to clarify where the shot is in relation to the space, if the background is nebulous or narrow in field of view.

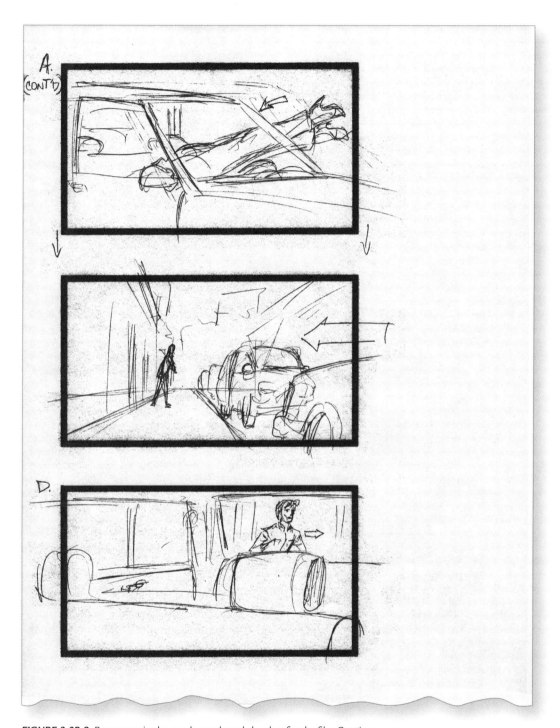

FIGURE 3.2B-9. Page seven in the rough storyboard sketches for the film *Overtime*.

```
INT. CAR - DAY

They're in pain, but too scared to move.

                    MICHELE
          Did he see us?


                    RACHEL
          I don't think so. Let me
          check.

She pulls out a compact and lifts the little
mirror above the dash.

In the mirror, the Man gets into his car.
```

Compare the lines of text from the script to the storyboard sketch in Figure 3.2b-10.

Commentary

The Director

Car scenes can be somewhat repetitive and boring to shoot since space is limited. In trying to come up with an interesting way to shoot Rachel and Michele in the car, I chose to use a high angle. This choice became accentuated by how the blocking worked out in rehearsal. The actors came up with the idea of Rachel rolling on top of Michele to scope out the agent on the street. This choice added to the humor of the scene while continuing to establish the relationship between Rachel and Michele.

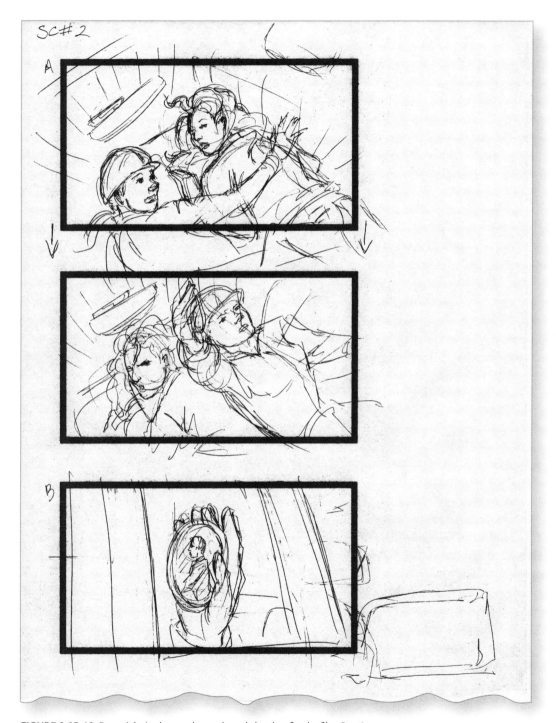

FIGURE 3.2B-10. Page eight in the rough storyboard sketches for the film *Overtime*.

```
                    RACHEL
          No. Thank god . . . Don't
          just lie there, follow
          him!

They straighten themselves out, Michele
fighting to keep the driver's seat.
```

Compare the lines of text from the script to the storyboard sketch in Figure 3.2b-11.

Commentary

The Storyboard Artist

Here, in the frame of Rachel and Michele sitting up in the car, I employ four methods of showing motion. The first is the use of successive frames for the single shot, second is the use of small arrows to indicate character movement, third is the use of a large arrow to indicate the car's movement, and finally, I used lines to indicate speed. It is up to the artist to combine whatever methods they feel fit to illustrate what is intended.

This blank frame indicates the end of the scene.

FIGURE 3.2B-11. Page nine in the rough storyboard sketches for the film *Overtime.*

```
EXT. DIVE BAR - DAY

The Man pulls up in front of the old bar
across the street. Michele and Rachel watch
him go in.
```

Compare the lines of text from the script to the storyboard sketch in Figure 3.2b-12.

Commentary

The Director
The location we secured doubled for the street location at the beginning of the film and the exterior of the bar. I chose to set this scene in the parking lot of the bar to avoid seeing too much of the surrounding area. This allowed us to make the most of our time and resources.

From a story perspective, I thought that having Rachel and Michele follow the agent at close proximity added to their character. It showed how inexperienced they are.

The Storyboard Artist
From a storytelling perspective, I exaggerated Rachel's crouched position so that just the top of her head and fingers are visible, to convey a comedic feel to the final frame on this page. Knowing that this is a comedy, and that the director will be drawing upon the humor of the actors, this frame subtly conveys the tone of the film.

FIGURE 3.2B-12. Page ten in the rough storyboard sketches for the film *Overtime*.

```
                    RACHEL
          Stay here. He'll notice
          you.


                    MICHELE
          Yeah, and you're going
          to blend into the
          woodwork in that getup
          -- or you have a spare
          dress stuffed in that
          belt?

     Smiling sweetly, Rachel reaches into a pocket
     - DRAGGING OUT A DRESS.
```

Compare the lines of text from the script to the storyboard sketch in Figure 3.2b-13.

Commentary

The Storyboard Artist

Rather than draw two separate frames to indicate the snap zoom at the bottom of the page, I chose to use arrows leading to a smaller frame. This saved time and conveyed the intention with greater clarity.

FIGURE 3.2B-13. Page 11 in the rough storyboard sketches for the film *Overtime*.

```
EXT. DIVE BAR -- MICHELE'S CAR - SAME DAY

An ODDLY DRESSED WOMAN with short hair gets
out of Michele's car.


                     RACHEL
           You keep watch, Michele.
```

Compare the lines of text from the script to the storyboard sketch in Figure 3.2b-14.

Commentary

The Director
During rehearsals, Ramona Taj, who plays Rachel, came up with the idea of wearing a sari, a traditional Indian dress, as the second disguise Rachel would wear in the film when she is undercover.

In the script Rachel reveals the dress to Michele as proof that she is always prepared. I wanted to show off Rachel's pride in her disguise by shooting her heroically. I chose to shoot her in slow motion and with a low angle to make her seem like a comic book character. The camera movement adds to the drama of the moment while adhering to the shooting strategy for Rachel's character.

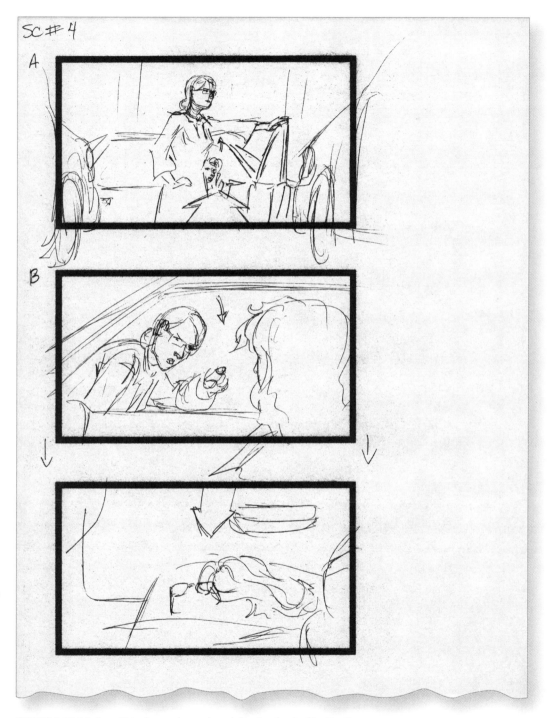

FIGURE 3.2B-14. Page 12 in the rough storyboard sketches for the film *Overtime*.

```
Rachel leaves, and Michele grabs the wig and
sunglasses Rachel left on the car seat.
```

Compare the lines of text from the script to the storyboard sketch in Figure 3.2b-15.

Commentary

The Storyboard Artist

Storytelling with images is done by utilizing many methods; juxtaposing frames, arrows, and also body language. If I draw a frame of a child looking innocent with their head cocked and juxtapose it with a frame of an adult looking cross while holding a broken lamp, it tells you that the adult is upset with the child, who is being coy about breaking the lamp. The artist should try to put as much body language and facial emotion into the frame as is called for to convey what is happening in the scene.

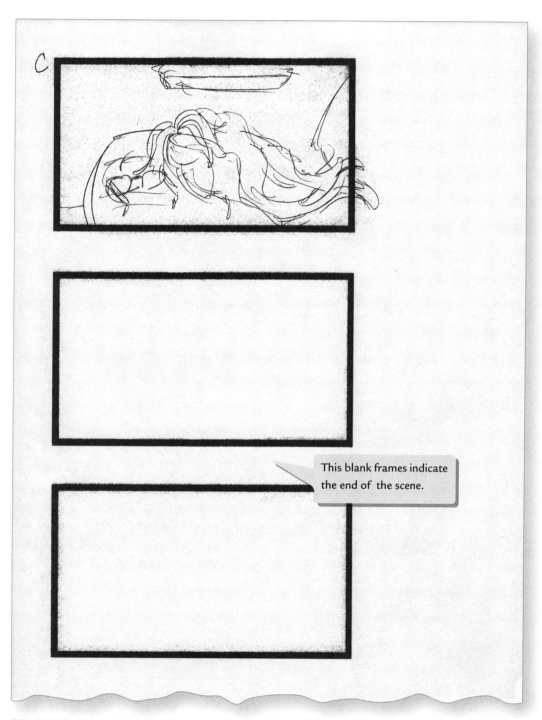

FIGURE 3.2B-15. Page 13 in the rough storyboard sketches for the film *Overtime*.

```
INT. DIVE BAR - SAME DAY

It's not too crowded. There are tables for
lunch, but nobody eating.

The Man is ordering some beers, so Rachel
leans against the end of the bar.

MICHELE walks in wearing Rachel's wig and
sunglasses! But she is acting tough enough to
frighten the men off.
```

Compare the lines of text from the script to the storyboard sketch in Figure 3.2b-16.

Commentary

The Director

For Michele's entrance into the bar I chose to contrast what I did with Rachel in the previous scene. When I revealed Rachel in her disguise, we sketched her like a comic book character. With the reveal of Michele's disguise I wanted to show her as a tough gal, a rebel, since she defied Rachel's order to stay put in the car. We sketched Michele in a static frame walking toward the camera. I wanted this shot to be in slow motion as well to heighten Michele's attitude as she entered in defiance.

NOTE   *Directors sometimes draw quick thumbnail sketches and give these sketches to the storyboard artist in addition to meeting with the artist to create the storyboard.*

FIGURE 3.2B-16. Page 14 in the rough storyboard sketches for the film *Overtime*.

Michele strides to the bar, standing next to
the Man -- without being recognized.

Rachel moves up from the end of the bar;
getting so close that the Man bumps her.

                    MAN
          Excuse me.

No hint of him recognizing Rachel. Rachel
thinks she is winning their game.

Then the Man spots Michele – instant
interest. Michele beams. Oh yeah, now Michele
is winning the game!

Door chimes ring. A MYSTERIOUS WOMAN (?)
enters the bar. She's sexy, tough -- and both
women hate her.

The Man grabs his beers and runs toward the
mysterious woman, leading her to a table.

Compare the lines of text from the script to the storyboard sketch in Figure
3.2b-17.

Commentary

The Storyboard Artist
Always try to capture the essence of the action of each shot in a dramatic
way, even if the shot and action happening within it are simple. For example,
I tried to give Illidia a devious look as she enters the second frame.

FIGURE 3.2B-17. Page 15 in the rough storyboard sketches for the film *Overtime*.

```
Rachel moves first, getting the closer table.
Michele settles for a table COVERED WITH
PLATES FROM THE PREVIOUS DINER.

As they watch, the Man and the Woman lean
close. She pushes her beer aside, whispers
something. The Man turns aside to grab the
beer back.


                    MAN
          Scotch, please, make it
          a double.
```

Compare the lines of text from the script to the storyboard sketch in Figure 3.2b-18.

Commentary

The Storyboard Artist

As stated earlier in the book, boards often are not ornately drawn. I kept the boards for this film rather simple. You'll notice the backgrounds are mostly implied with loose lines. This reflects the needs and capabilities of the production. The boards needed to be turned around quickly, and since there weren't many specific sets, props, or wardrobe that needed elaboration, the simplicity of the boards works for this film. Some productions with specific or elaborate details like period, sci-fi, or fantasy films may require more detail to depict the world being portrayed. In cases like this, more time has to be allotted to the storyboard artist so they can properly render the world.

FIGURE 3.2B-18. Page 16 in the rough storyboard sketches for the film *Overtime*.

```
While the man is distracted, the Woman
sprinkles powder into his beer.

Both Michele and Rachel sit up, alert - but
are afraid of blowing their cover!
```

Compare the lines of text from the script to the storyboard sketch in Figure 3.2b-19.

Commentary

The Director

For the poisoning scene I knew that I wanted lots of tension while still carrying over the comedic tone of the film. The comedy would come from the scenario and the acting, but the tension must come from the editing. In thumbnail sketches I drew most of the scene with close ups that I could intercut to build the tension through the edit. The intimacy of the close-up forces the audience to be further immersed in the action of the scene and the drama of each character.

The Storyboard Artist

I try to talk to the director about how they intend to cut a scene. Usually general notes are given regarding how the shots should be arranged or repeated. Once complete, the director will look at the arrangement to make sure it is telling the story as they intended. If it is not, revisions will be made. This scene is a good example of how storyboarding can help a director figure out how they want to edit the footage.

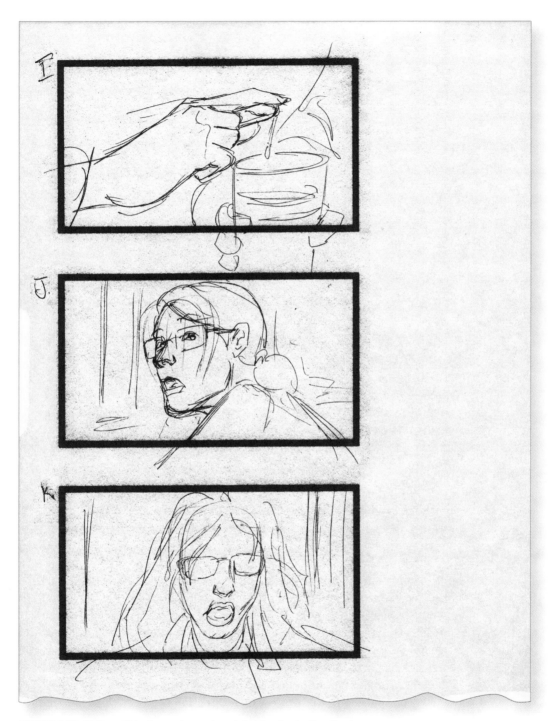

FIGURE 3.2B-19. Page 17 in the rough storyboard sketches for the film *Overtime*.

```
Panicked, Michele forks a bit of food and
FLINGS IT at the man. It lands in his beer!

The man looks over, and Michele acts
innocent.

They go back to talking until the chicken
wings arrive.
```

Compare the lines of text from the script to the storyboard sketch in Figure 3.2b-20.

Commentary

The Storyboard Artist

Screen direction is another subject that can get tricky. You always want to make sure that the frames you are drawing have proper screen direction. For example, when you have two people talking and you are covering each person in separate shots, you want to make sure that the people are facing each other when the shots are intercut in editing.

The 180 degree rule is used to make sure that proper screen direction is employed. Draw a line between the positions of the two characters, then keep your camera angles on one side of the line. Generally this is easily achieved with only two characters present in the scene. But when you start to get into multiple characters and then add character movement to the equation, like in this bar scene, it can get complicated. In situations like this, it is good to rely on the overhead diagram to plot out the character movements. This is especially true if you are feeling unsure about the screen direction. Once the characters' movements are plotted, establish 180 degree lines between the characters or subjects who are interacting with each other. Then, keep all your camera angles on one side of the line when drawing your coverage. This way you can make sure that your screen direction is correct for your frames.

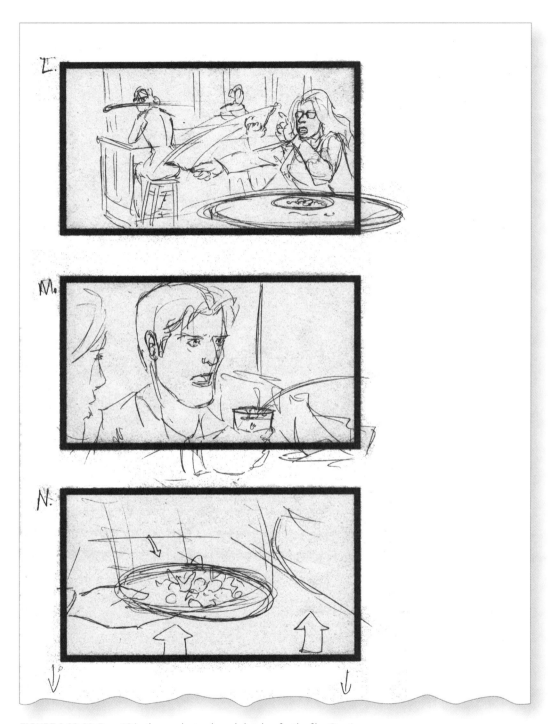

FIGURE 3.2B-20. Page 18 in the rough storyboard sketches for the film *Overtime*.

```
AT THE TABLE the Woman talks in the Man's
ear, trying to hold his gaze while her hand
SPRINKLES more powder onto the chicken wings.

Then she gives Michele a cold stare while the
Man picks up a chicken wing.
```

Compare the lines of text from the script to the storyboard sketch in Figure 3.2b-21.

Commentary

The Storyboard Artist

The storyboard artist needs to be able to understand filmmaking. While this project was broken down into shots before the boards were made, that's not always the case. Sometimes the director is still trying to work out how they want to tell the story and in some cases the director may be at a loss on exactly how they want to convey a scene. In instances like this it may fall on the artist to come up with suggestions on how a scene can be translated into visuals. The artist needs to be prepared to create visuals that match the style and tone of the script. When boarding for other directors I always prefer them to be as prepared as possible with clear intentions and a detailed shot list. This allows for the boarding process to be quick and usually requires few revisions.

FIGURE 3.2B-21. Page 19 in the rough storyboard sketches for the film *Overtime*.

They're both panicked, but what to do?

Rachel grabs a bottle of ketchup.

He raises the chicken wing toward his
mouth to take a bite.

Rachel squirts ketchup all over the Man's
face!

Compare the lines of text from the script to the storyboard sketch in Figure
3.2b-22.

Commentary

The Director
Once Rachel decides to squirt the agent, the danger of the poisoning and the
resulting tension is broken.

I chose to have the storyboard artist board the end of the scene with wider
shots to help relieve the tension visually.

FIGURE 3.2B-22. Page 20 in the rough storyboard sketches for the film *Overtime*.

Spitting, the Man wipes it off and leaps
to his feet.

                    MAN

         You want a piece of
         me?

                  RACHEL

         Yeah! Yeah, I – sorta
         do.

                    MAN

         Do I know you?

                  WOMAN

         Honey, let's just get
         out of here.

Michele leaps to her feet – knocking over
the small table where she was sitting.

                  MICHELE

         Illidia? Illidia
         Snow!

The Woman pauses nonchalantly then knocks
Michele into her seat and heads for the
back. The Man is torn between fighting
Rachel and following his sweetheart -
which allows Michele to chase after her.

Compare the lines of text from the script to the storyboard sketch in Figure 3.2b-23.

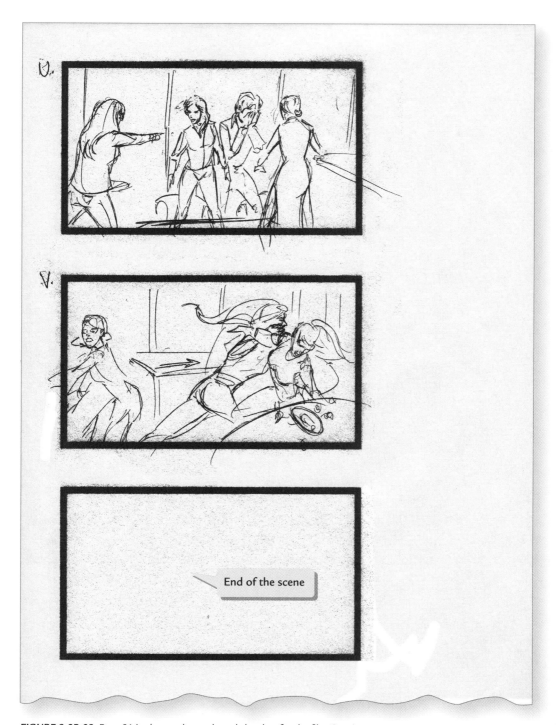

End of the scene

FIGURE 3.2B-23. Page 21 in the rough storyboard sketches for the film *Overtime*.

```
EXT. DIVE BAR - SAME DAY

Michele bursts out of the door - there's
nobody there. The woman has vanished.
```

Compare the lines of text from the script to the storyboard sketch in Figure 3.2b-24.

Commentary

The Director

For the opening of the fight scene, I chose to break the camera strategy of static frames that I employed with Michele throughout the film. I decided to go with a sweeping camera move to show Michele's shift into "action mode" and to signify the beginning of the impending fight.

FIGURE 3.2B-24. Page 22 in the rough storyboard sketches for the film *Overtime.*

```
The back door opens. Michele spins around and
Illidia catches her, and throws Michele to
the ground.
```

Compare the lines of text from the script to the storyboard sketch in Figure 3.2b-25.

Commentary

The Director

For the fight sequence I knew that I wanted to shoot it handheld, with the feel of the action sequences of the Bourne films. I wanted the action to feel raw and chaotic, peppered with reaction shots for comedy and close-ups for dialogue. So, I elected to thumbnail sketch the fight sequence sparsely to show general camera angles that would cover the action of the fight, and frames that would show coverage for reaction shots and dialogue. I did this because I knew that the best way to get footage that looked real and chaotic was to have a general plan of attack, but then to simply react to what we see in the fight as if we were bystanders trying to watch.

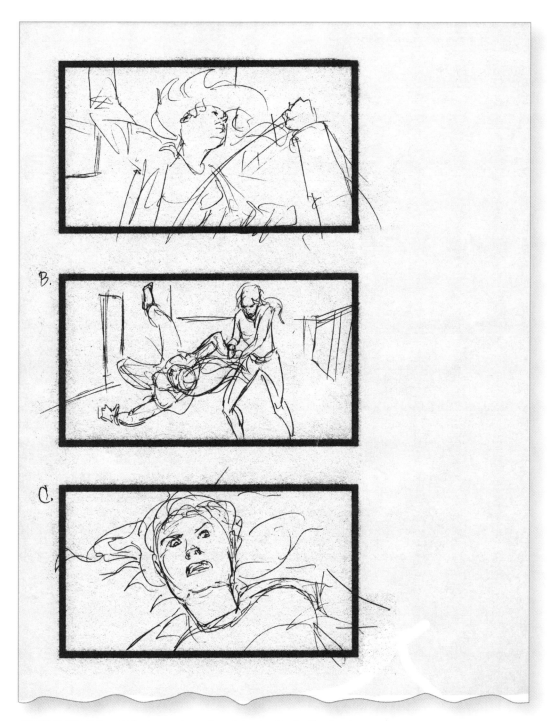

FIGURE 3.2B-25. Page 23 in the rough storyboard sketches for the film *Overtime*.

```
                    ILLIDIA
          Michele Estavanti, you
          stole my boyfriend.
          Prepare to die!

Illidia lifts her hand to strike. From
behind, Rachel grabs it!
```

Compare the lines of text from the script to the storyboard sketch in Figure 3.2b-26.

Commentary

The Storyboard Artist

Since I knew that most of the fight scene was going to be captured live on the set, aside from certain beats that wanted to be boarded, I did not have to go too far into boarding many of the details of the fight. I had choreography video of the fight as a reference for the boards. However, had the shooting strategy for the fight been different, and were I required to draw the scene, it could have taken many pages of frames to convey. On large movies especially, when the script calls for lots of action, multiple storyboard artists are hired to complete the work.

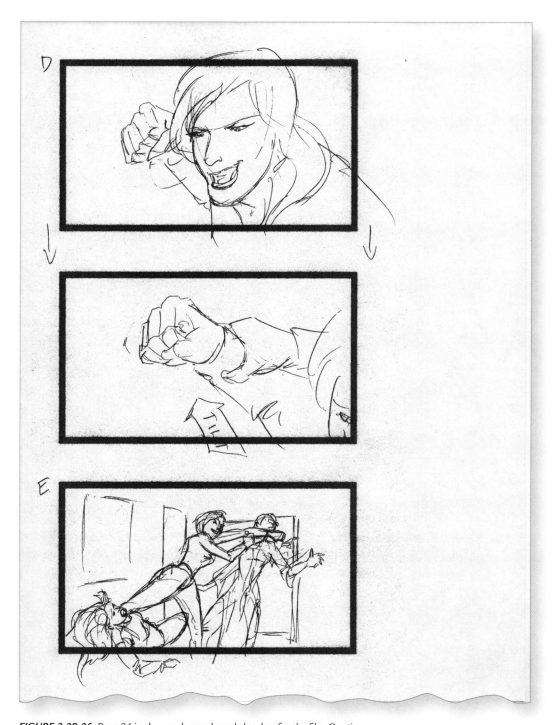

FIGURE 3.2B-26. Page 24 in the rough storyboard sketches for the film *Overtime*.

Two against one – it is unfair odds. Illidia
counters Rachel's every move while knocking
Michele down every time she attempts to get
up. Illidia is having fun.

Police lights dance across the wall. They all
turn, look into the light, and find the Man
standing there.

                    MAN
          Illidia Snow, you're
          under arrest.

Compare the lines of text from the script to the storyboard sketch in Figure
3.2b-27.

Commentary

The Director

The close-ups here illustrate my intentions for finding moments that may
be humorous within the fight sequence. I hope to find moments that are
humorous in different ways. The goal is to have Rachel's close-ups reveal
her utter surprise and worry over how badly Illidia is beating her. Michele's
close-ups will contrast Rachel's by showing her sheer frustration that she's
powerless to do anything to Illidia.

FIGURE 3.2B-27. Page 25 in the rough storyboard sketches for the film *Overtime*.

ILLIDIA

Honey . . . lose my
number!

She throws both Rachel and Michele toward
the Man and is gone before anybody can get to
their feet. A plain clothes agent chases after
Illidia.

MAN

What are you two doing
here?

MICHELE

Rachel dared me to come
here dressed like this.

MAN

But – how did you know
that was Illidia?

MICHELE

She made high school
living hell.

Compare the lines of text from the script to the storyboard sketch in Figure
3.2b-28.

Commentary

The Storyboard Artist

Trying to capture the peak moments of movement is generally important
when drawing action. The point just after an impact is a good place to start.
The frame of Illidia throwing Rachel depicts the moment just after she is
released, freezing the action in time, and setting up the next impact.

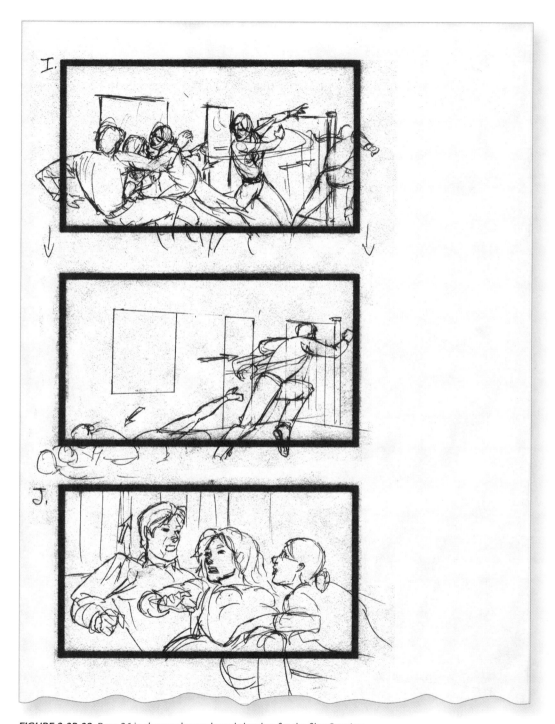

I.

J.

FIGURE 3.2B-28. Page 26 in the rough storyboard sketches for the film *Overtime.*

MAN

Go home and stay out
of trouble. Let the
professionals handle
this – Oh, and thank
you. Good to know you
have my back.

The Man runs off. Michele and Rachel finally
relax – or just plain collapse.

RACHEL

We have GOT to stop
stalking him! It isn't
healthy.

MICHELE

Are you kidding? Our
stalking saved his life!

Compare the lines of text from the script to the storyboard sketch in Figure 3.2b-29.

Commentary

The Director

For the final portion of the film I wanted to slow things down to allow the audience to take in the twist of the story; the reveal that Rachel and Michele are really just office assistants. I chose to go with static coverage to allow the dialogue and the acting to carry the film to a close.

FIGURE 3.2B-29. Page 27 in the rough storyboard sketches for the film *Overtime*.

```
                    RACHEL
          HE'S the FBI agent.
          We're just office
          assistants.


                    MICHELE
          We're more than that.
          We're better than that!

     But they aren't, and they know it.
```

Compare the lines of text from the script to the storyboard sketch in Figure 3.2b-30.

Commentary

The Storyboard Artist

The final shots between Rachel and Michele were drawn in a simple fashion to convey the slower pace intended in the direction for the final interchange between Rachel Michele. It is good to always try to find ways to communicate the director's vision in whatever way you can, even if it is small. I chose to draw their messy hair and weary smiles to convey what they went through in the film and the seeming bond that they now share.

FIGURE 3.2B-30. Page 28 in the rough storyboard sketches for the film *Overtime*.

Overtime

SHOT LIST

<u>SC#1</u>

A- MS- City Street, Camera **GLIDES** tilted toward the ground revealing high heels in full stride. We tilt up to reveal Rachel wearing overalls and carry a utility bag. We swing OTS and continue to track with her capturing her rhythmic step. She trips. (MASTER)–Rachel settles at the corner and ruffles through her utility bag. She looks up at window checks her watch then spots a familiar car pulling up. Rachel turns away then walks to the car, talks to Michele and jumps in as the Man exits building. Car follows Man.

A1 MCU- Rachel's Face as she walks.

B- MS (OTS)- Rachel pops down into driver's side window, scares Michele.

C- MS (OTS)- Michele.

D- FS- Man (from inside car)

<u>SC#2</u>

A- 2SHOT *(dutch)*- Rachel and Michele scrunched in car.

B- CU Mirror (HH)- CAM pushing in.

C- 2SHOT (Pass window)- Rachel and Michele untangle themselves, pop up & drive off.

<u>SC#3</u>

A- WS (*low angle*)- EXT BAR, CAM **GLIDES** off a parked car as the Man's car pulls into lot. Michele's car pulls in and lingers behind.

A1-2 SHOT- Rachel and Michele in car.

B- 2SHOT (behind car)- Rachel and Michele watch the Man enter the bar.

C- INSERT – Man entering Bar.

D- MCU – **SNAP ZOOM** as Rachel reveals clothes.

FIGURE 3.2C-1. The first page of the shot list including scenes one through three.

For this section we compare the shot list to the individual storyboard frames. In the second scene we start to see why storyboards could sometimes be used as shot lists, and why it is helpful to have storyboards in addition to your shot list. For example, the positioning of the actors and the camera in shot *SC#2 - A - 2SHOT (dutch) - Rachel and Michele scrunched in car* is unclear when reading the shot list description. Now look at Figure 3.2c-7. In an instant, the storyboard frame was able to capture the type of shot as well as the actors' and camera's positioning in the style the director imagined.

FIGURE 3.2C-2. Shot SC#1 - A.

FIGURE 3.2C-3. Shot SC#1 - A1.

FIGURE 3.2C-4. Shot SC#1 - B.

FIGURE 3.2C-5. Shot SC#1 - C.

FIGURE 3.2C-6. Shot SC#1 - D.

FIGURE 3.2C-7. Shot SC#2 - A.

FIGURE 3.2C-8. Shot SC#2 - B.

FIGURE 3.2C-9. Shot SC#2 - C.

FIGURE 3.2C-10. Shot SC#3 - A.

FIGURE 3.2C-11. Shot SC#3 - A1.

FIGURE 3.2C-12. Shot SC#3 - B.

FIGURE 3.2C-13. Shot SC#3 - C.

FIGURE 3.2C-14. Shot SC#3 - D.

SC#4 – EXT BAR – MOMENTS LATER

A- FS (*slo mo*)- CAM, low angle, ***SLIDES*** in as Rachel exits car.

B- MS (OTS)- Rachel drops into pass window. Tilt down to reveal wig and glasses.

C- CU- Wig and glasses.

SC#5 – INT BAR- DAY

A- WS (MASTER)- Rachel walks up to bar as the Man orders a drink at bar. Michele enters and walks to the bar. Rachel moves closer and bumps man. Woman enters everyone sits.

B- CU- beer slams on bar counter.

C- MS (*slo mo*)- Michele enters bar.

D- 3 SHOT- Rachel notices Michele enter. Michele takes position next to Man. Cover to when Michele sits at table.

E- MS- CAM ***SLIDES*** as Ilidia enters bar and meets with Man. He leads her to table.

F- WS- Man moves to table with Ilidia.

G- 2 SHOT- Man and Ilidia sit.

H- CU- Ilidia at table. Tilt to reveal her powdering wings.

I- CU- Ilidia puts powder in Man's drink.

J- CU – Rachel

K- CU- Michele

L- CU- Man at table

M- WS- They stand. Ilidia knocks Michele over and exits.

FIGURE 3.2C-31. The second page of the shot list, including scenes four and five.

FIGURE 3.2C-15. Shot SC#4 - A.

FIGURE 3.2C-16. Shot SC#4 - B.

FIGURE 3.2C-17. Shot SC#4 - C.

FIGURE 3.2C-18. Shot SC#5 - A.

FIGURE 3.2C-19. Shot SC#5 - B.

FIGURE 3.2C-20. Shot SC#5 - C.

FIGURE 3.2C-21. Shot SC#5 - D.

FIGURE 3.2C-22. Shot SC#5 - E.

FIGURE 3.2C-23. Shot SC#5 - F.

FIGURE 3.2C-24. Shot SC#5 - G.

FIGURE 3.2C-25. Shot SC#5 - H - With reveal.

FIGURE 3.2C-26. Shot SC#5 - I.

FIGURE 3.2C-27. Shot SC#5 - J.

FIGURE 3.2C-28. Shot SC#5 - K.

FIGURE 3.2C-29. Shot SC#5 - L.

FIGURE 3.2C-30. Shot SC#5 - M.

Storyboards translate the script into visual elements by using drawn pictures, while the shot list does so using text. Positioning of the cast in relation to the camera and the surroundings are communicated in the shot list, but are shown visually and with greater clarity in the storyboard. Where the storyboard surpasses the shot list is in it's ability show where the characters are in space, how the shots relate to each other, what the characters' emotions are—in other words, storytelling.

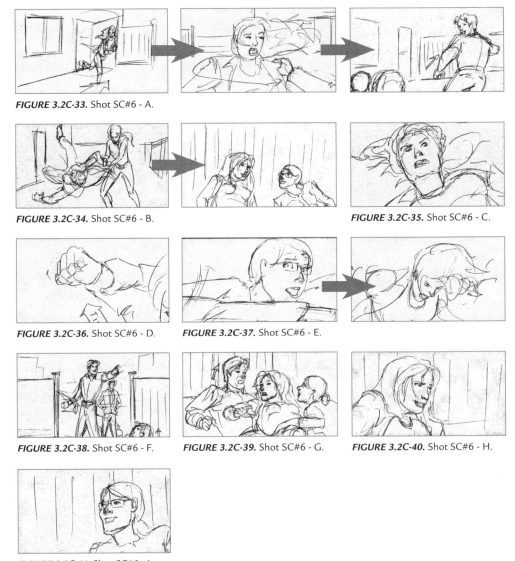

FIGURE 3.2C-33. Shot SC#6 - A.

FIGURE 3.2C-34. Shot SC#6 - B.

FIGURE 3.2C-35. Shot SC#6 - C.

FIGURE 3.2C-36. Shot SC#6 - D.

FIGURE 3.2C-37. Shot SC#6 - E.

FIGURE 3.2C-38. Shot SC#6 - F.

FIGURE 3.2C-39. Shot SC#6 - G.

FIGURE 3.2C-40. Shot SC#6 - H.

FIGURE 3.2C-41. Shot SC#6 - I.

<u>**SC#6 – EXT BAR – CONTINUOUS**</u>

A- FS (MASTER)- CAM *GLIDES* in as Michele storms out of the bar. Swing around to behind Michele to reveal Ilidia gone. Ilidia steps into frame and fight ensues with Rachel entering. The Man comes and Illidia escapes. Rachel and Michele are victorious.

B- WS- Fight - Illidia throws Rachel and Michele at Man and escapes. Man says thanks.

C- CU- Michele on ground.

D- CU- Illidia- Tilt up to Illidia's hand as she's about to strike. Rachel grabs Illidia.

E- MCU- Fight, float between Rachel & Michele

F- FS- Man

G- 3SHOT- Rachel, Man and Michele. Cover through end of scene.

H- CU- Michele

I- CU- Rachel

FIGURE 3.2C-32. The last page of the shot list including scene six. The final scene.

Commentary

The Storyboard Artist

When translating storyboards from a shot list, it is always important to review each shot with the director to clarify what is intended. Shot lists are often written in the director's shorthand, and elements of the shot can be missed or misunderstood if the list is not clarified. When you meet with a director, be sure to ask questions about anything that is unclear, and always summarize your understanding of the shot so that you are certain both of you are on the same page. If you are boarding your own work, try to make sure that the corresponding shot list is clear and concise for all involved.

3.2d - Location and talent photographs to storyboard comparison

The following figures are a comparison between location photographs or screen shots of the cast to the final storyboard. There is a close resemblance between the photographs and the boards. This enables the director and crew to accurately see what the camera will film.

In Figures 3.2d-1 and 3.2d-11 the location photographs show a bar with rounded edges on one side and rounded smaller tables on the other side. The storyboard artist was able to capture this look effectively in Figures 3.2d-2 and 3.2d-12, allowing the director to clearly see the shot in the location where filming will take place.

Consider Figures 3.2d-10, for example. This sketch includes three cast members standing at the bar. In one glance, because of the detail in the drawing, it is clear what the positioning is for each actor, who they are, the props they are using, and their wardrobes.

Commentary

The Storyboard Artist
In keeping with the idea that storyboards should be as close to the filmed image as possible, it is important to capture the likeness of the actors and locations while drawing. Although boards with less detail will work for a production, the closer you can draw the image to the actual intent of the film, the easier it will be for the person looking at the boards to visualize the story.

Boards are usually done in great volume. In the interest of time, the frames drawn should capture a likeness while being simple enough to allow the artist the ability to keep up with the work load.

FIGURE 3.2D-1. Inside bar.

FIGURE 3.2D-2. Inside bar sketched

FIGURE 3.2D-3. Ramona Taj.

FIGURE 3.2D-4. Ramona Taj sketched.

FIGURE 3.2D-5. Leighsa Burgin.

FIGURE 3.2D-6. Leighsa Burgin sketched.

FIGURE 3.2D-7. Alisha Finneran.

FIGURE 3.2D-8. Alisha Finneran sketched.

FIGURE 3.2D-9. Fiore Leo.

FIGURE 3.2D-10. Fiore Leo sketched.

FIGURE 3.2D-11. Inside bar.

FIGURE 3.2D-12. Inside bar sketched

3.2e - Prop and wardrobe photographs to storyboard comparison

For this project, the props were predominantly everyday items. There were, however, a few props that were unusual. Photographs of these props are helpful for the storyboard artist for the creation of the storyboards. The more imagery available to the artist, the closer the storyboards will resemble how the story will unfold through the eyes of the camera.

The ornate Indian-style dress in Figure 3.2e-9 is clearly represented in the sketch in Figure 3.2e-10. It helps to define a prop and get a feel for the character. In Figure 3.2e-8 the car matching the photograph of the car in Figure 3.2e-7 gives the feel of the scene.

Commentary

The Storyboard Artist

In addition to photographs, sometimes the artist will go to the location to see it and get a feel for it in person. Models can also be used by the storyboard artist for locations or for characters that may be created by effects teams. All of these tools can help the artist in creating the likeness of the world that will be filmed.

FIGURE 3.2E-1. Photograph of the high heels.

FIGURE 3.2E-.2. Drawing of the high heels.

FIGURE 3.2E-3. Photograph of the hard hat.

FIGURE 3.2E-4. Drawing of the hard hat.

FIGURE 3.2E-5. The sunglasses and wig props.

FIGURE 3.2E-6. Drawing of sunglasses and wig.

FIGURE 3.2E-7. Photograph of the car.

FIGURE 3.2E-8. Drawing of the front of the car.

FIGURE 3.2E-9. Photograph of the dress.

FIGURE 3.2E-10. Drawing of the dress.

SUMMARY

The storyboard is the film in illustration form. *Overtime* is used as an example of the process of making storyboards on an actual project. The focus is on how storyboards affect a film from preproduction to its final cut. The chapter also includes information concerning all the elements gathered by the storyboard artist in preproduction. The use of side-by-side storyboard comparisons, together with accompanying point-of-view commentaries, shows the initial steps of translating the script into images and demonstrates the importance of storyboards. Scouting for a location or building a set creates the visual environment for the storytelling. Props or wardrobe images or descriptions will help the storyboards to closely depict how the objects will look when filmed. The director provides the overall vision and storytelling style of the project.

REVIEW QUESTIONS: CHAPTER 3

1. Who gathers information and how is it gathered for the storyboard?

2. What does the director do when he first gets a script? Explain the process in detail.

3. Why are location diagrams and photographs important?

4. Why is it important to map as much of the film in storyboards as possible?

5. Why is it important to have both a storyboard and a shot list?

DISCUSSION / ESSAY QUESTIONS

1. Keep a journal recalling important information from the text and ideas of how to use the information when making your own storyboard.

2. Summarize each section of the book and discuss the parts that would be most helpful.

3. Discuss or write about any personal experience you have had, or movie you have watched, using what you have learned from the book.

4. After a short story or script is read, develop storyboards to go with it.

5. After reading the unmarked script, discuss how you would have broken down the story into scenes.

APPLYING WHAT YOU HAVE LEARNED

1. Make a common preproduction storyboard time-line sample.

2. Develop a short story and draw a storyboard for the story.

3. Create a shot list for the story.

4. Film a scene based on one of your storyboards.

5. Watch a movie. Pick a short segment of the movie and write a shot list for that segment.

6. Watch a movie. Pick a short segment of the movie and draw a storyboard of that segment.

CHAPTER 4

Production

OVERVIEW AND LEARNING OBJECTIVES

In this chapter:

- 4.1 - Day of the shoot of the short film, *Overtime*
- 4.2 - Storyboard-to-actual shot comparison
- 4.3 - Updated boards because of on-set changes
- 4.4 - The shot list-to-film comparison
- 4.5 - Cast and crew credits for *Overtime*

4.1 - Day of the shoot of the short film, *Overtime*

In this chapter we will cover the events that occurred during the two-day shoot for the film, *Overtime*. This short film is shown in its entirety on the DVD. We will compare the storyboards to screen shots from the short film, cover on-set changes, and compare the shot list to the actual shots. We provide animated, side-by-side comparisons on the accompanying DVD.

The goal of this chapter is for you to see through the eyes of the people working on the project (Figure 4.1). The sections that compare storyboards with the corresponding film stills will include commentaries from the various cast and crew members. We included these different viewpoints in order to illustrate how different departments will use the storyboards for different reasons.

For example, while the director of photography will use the storyboards to help set up the proper shot, the sound recordist might use them to plan what mikes should be used and where they should be placed so that the mikes are not seen in the frame. One of the most important people to use the storyboards will be the script supervisor. The script supervisor uses the boards to

FIGURE 4.1. This photograph is part of the opening shot sequence. The camera movement for the shot is shown in the overhead location diagram in Section 3.1c.

help keep track of what shots have been completed in order to be sure that a scene is covered properly. Actors might use the boards to find out where the cameras will be so they can mentally rehearse before shooting starts.

4.2 - Storyboard-to-actual shot comparison

The following section compares the final storyboards to the final cut of the film. These comparisons are a bridge between what was conceived in pre-production, opposed to what actually was shot on set. You will find the storyboard comparisons to the completed short film, *Overtime*, on the accompanying DVD.

You will see that the following storyboards are different than the quick sketches depicted in the previous chapter. In Chapter 3 we learned that, in the early phases of preproduction, the boards are used to test shot ideas for scenes from the script. At that point, it is not necessary to spend time finalizing the artwork when there is such a high probability that changes might be made. Once the director is satisfied with the sketches, the artist can fully complete the boards (Figure 4.2-1).

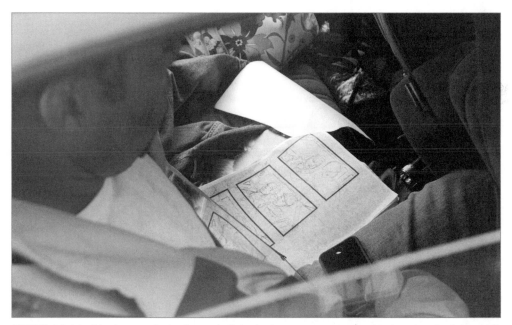

FIGURE 4.2-1. In this photograph, the director is sitting in the prop car overseeing the shot where Rachel and Michele are confronting each other in the front seat. The storyboards are being used as a reference.

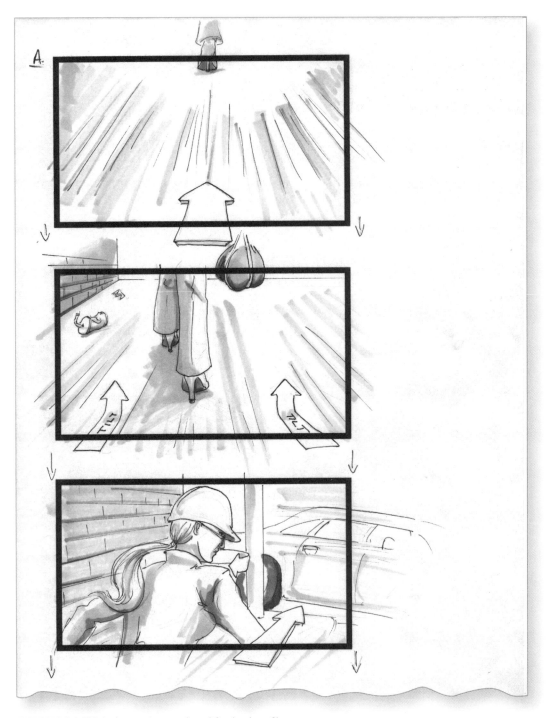

FIGURE 4.2-2. This is the opening storyboard for the short film.

FIGURE 4.2-2A. The opening scene for the short film and our first look at Rachel's high heels.

FIGURE 4.2-2B. The camera is tilting up to reveal more of Rachel as she walks.

FIGURE 4.2-2C. The camera is now moving in front of Rachel in order to show a hard hat as well as the heels.

Compare the storyboard page (Figure 4.2-2) to fames from the short film (Figures 4.2-2a – 4.2-2c).

Commentary

The Director

While filming, this shot did not work out the way it was boarded. When I originally conceived it I wanted it to be one long camera move that would introduce us to Rachel and lead us all the way up to the point where she confronts Michele in the car. My idea was for the camera to reveal Rachel, starting from her heels and continuing to move with her as she made her way through the scene. I wanted the opening to be dynamic so that the energy would come from the interplay between Rachel and the camera. On shoot day, it ended up having to be broken into different shots.

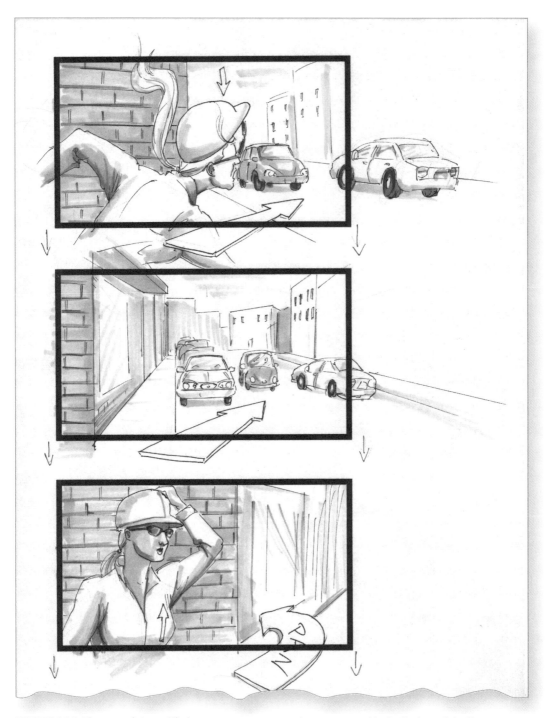

FIGURE 4.2-3. The arrows bring to life the camera movements and are represented in the final cut of the film.

FIGURE 4.2-3A. In this scene, the camera is more stationary rather than moving around Rachel. This is an example of the final shot being close to, but not an exact duplication of, the storyboards because of on-location adjustments.

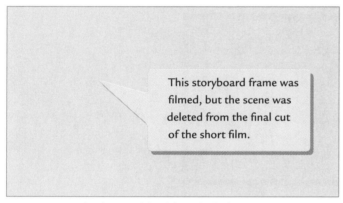

This storyboard frame was filmed, but the scene was deleted from the final cut of the short film.

FIGURE 4.2-3B. The shot was deleted from the final cut.

FIGURE 4.2-3C. This shot varied slightly from the storyboard in order to show the phone repair equipment. The camera movement is the same, however.

Compare the storyboard page (Figure 4.2-3) to frames from the short film (Figures 4.2-3a – 4.2-3c).

Commentary

The Director

This type of shot would best be done with a steadicam. It being a low-budget production, we were not able to rent the equipment necessary, so we built a camera stabilizer or 'poor man's steadicam.' Unfortunately, the restriction of the stabilizer and our lack of time prevented us from truly capturing the shot as precisely as I wanted it. I decided to cover the scene with other angles to assure we maintained the highest quality and production value. As a result, you will notice multiple shots in the film that are different from the boards. This is fairly common. Things do not always work out on set the way you intend them to, so having a backup plan and the ability to improvise are important.

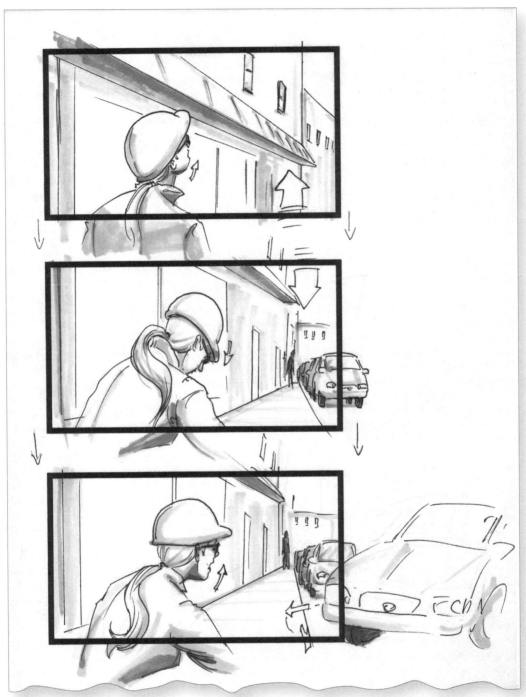

FIGURE 4.2-4. This storyboard was changed just a little, with the car pulling up on the other side of the road to reflect the updated shot.

FIGURE 4.2-4A. This shot was inserted in editing.

FIGURE 4.2-4B. An over-the-shoulder (OTS) shot of Michele's car.

FIGURE 4.2-4C. Rachel sees a car that she knows, parking in front of the building.

Compare the storyboard page (Figure 4.2-4) to frames from the short film (Figures 4.2-4a – 4.2-4c).

Commentary

The Director

Even though we did not get this shot the way we wanted to, our coverage did allow for some good cutting points that actually added to the humor of the scene. Sometimes things work in your favor and in this instance they did.

The Producer

The street we originally scouted was a main street, which we decided to be too busy, and we needed to find an alternate location for the opening sequence. The location we chose has multiple alleys and side streets, which made it ideal. For safety reasons while on set, we also decided to change the position of the car in the shot. On a larger production, a change like this could have been re-boarded for cohesiveness.

FIGURE 4.2-5. Storyboard number four in the film sequence and our first look at Michele.

FIGURE 4.2-5A. Rachel trying to hide from Michele.

FIGURE 4.2-5B. Rachel crossing the street and walking around Michele's car from behind.

FIGURE 4.2-5C. Michele parking and trying to look inconspicuous.

Compare the storyboard page (Figure 4.2-5) to frames from the short film (Figures 4.2-5a – 4.2-5c).

Commentary

The Sound Recordist
Storyboards make it much easier for me to be the "invisible person" on set. I can anticipate what the shot will need, sound-wise, and have the gear ready to move in when I have the OK, plus I will already have a good idea how to keep out of frame once the camera is in place.

FIGURE 4.2-6. Storyboard number five. The B in the upper-left side of the page indicates that this is the start of shot B.

FIGURE 4.2-6A. A close-up (CU) of Michele.

FIGURE 4.2-6B. A close-up (CU) of Rachel.

FIGURE 4.2-6C. Michele not impressed with Rachel's story.

Compare the storyboard page (Figure 4.2-6) to frames from the short film (Figures 4.2-6a – 4.2-6c).

Commentary

Cast Member

When I am handed storyboards on set, it helps me put everything together. The problem when I am just looking at a script is that it is a very flat way of looking at my part and the scene. The boards bring that other dimension. I get to see where everything is in relationship with each other and in relation with the camera. I get to see through the eyes of the director just a little bit more, and that helps me with my performance.

FIGURE 4.2-7. Storyboard number six. This first stunt of the film takes place when Rachel dives into the car.

FIGURE 4.2-7A. A close-up (CU) of Rachel.

FIGURE 4.2-7B. A close-up (CU) of Michele.

FIGURE 4.2-7C. This shot was filmed in the way it is shown on the storyboard, but was edited out in postproduction.

Compare the storyboard page (Figure 4.2-7) to frames from the short film (Figures 4.2-7a – 4.2-7c).

Commentary

The Director
For the shot where Rachel dives into the car, I originally wanted the camera inside the car and to pull back as she leapt toward it. After trying out the move in rehearsal, our director of photography and I decided the gag would work best if we did it on a cut, so we left the camera static and allowed the energy to come from Rachel's movement. This allowed the motion to be quickened in editing and made for funnier action in the film.

FIGURE 4.2-8. Storyboard number seven in the production.

FIGURE 4.2-8A. Rachel's feet, after the dive.

FIGURE 4.2-8B. Our first glimpse of The Man.

FIGURE 4.2-8C. The Man is unaware that he is being watched.

Compare the storyboard page (Figure 4.2-8) to frames from the short film (Figures 4.2-8a – 4.2-8c).

Commentary

The Director

After watching the rehearsal, we also chose to add a couple of different angles on Rachel's legs diving into the car that might work better for the cut. This straight-on close-up worked the best in editing.

FIGURE 4.2-9. Storyboard number eight in the production and the start of scene two.

FIGURE 4.2-9A. The crowded front seat of the car.

FIGURE 4.2-9B. Rachel shows off her spy skills.

FIGURE 4.2-9C. The Man, seen in the compact mirror.

Compare the storyboard page (Figure 4.2-9) to frames from the short film (Figures 4.2-9a – 4.2-9c).

Commentary

The Director
The shot of the FBI agent in the reflection of Rachel's compact mirror was intended to be a camera move toward the compact as the agent stepped into the reflection. This was another shot, as simple as it seems, that proved difficult to get. Three individual points of motion had to be coordinated: the camera, the actor operating the compact (who in actuality could not see the agent in the reflection) and the agent. The timing of the move proved so difficult that we had to shoot it in two pieces; the compact being lifted up in search of the agent, and the compact finding the agent. The director of photography ended up using a snap-zoom to add camera "movement" to the shot.

This blank frame indicates the end of the scene.

FIGURE 4.2-10. Storyboard number nine in the production and the end of scene two.

FIGURE 4.2-10A. Michele ready to follow The Man.

FIGURE 4.2-10B. Rachel pops up beside Michele.

Compare the storyboard page (Figure 4.2-10) to frames from the short film (Figures 4.2-10a – 4.2-10c).

Commentary

The Director of Photography

On-set, there are parts of the day where the schedule might get hectic or we lose track of where we are; shooting is like we are in the center of a tornado. It is really nice to have the boards to go back to like a map. They are a great skeleton for the movie, a great center of gravity for that tornado that is production.

Storyboards, as a tool used by director, cast, and crew members, help to maintain organization amid the frantic activity on set.

BRIEF REVIEW OF TERMS:

BLOCK / BLOCKING to plan or rehearse to work out the movement of the camera and placement of the cast and crew during a shot or scene.

DIRECTOR OF PHOTOGRAPHY (DP) A movie photographer who is in charge of shooting the movie and is responsible for achieving artistic and technical decisions related to the image.

FIGURE 4.2-11. Storyboard number ten in the production and the beginning of scene three.

FIGURE 4.2-11A. The Man's car arriving at a bar.

FIGURE 4.2-11B. Rachel and Michele's car following.

FIGURE 4.2-11C. Rachel and Michele stopping in front of the bar.

Compare the storyboard page (Figure 4.2-11) to frames from the short film (Figures 4.2-11a – 4.2-11c).

Commentary

The Director
The boarded shot for the opening of this scene got scrapped entirely. The director of photography wanted to get something that gave us a better establishing shot. Not to mention that the camera move was proving to be too long and would have taken up too much screen time for the quick-paced film we were trying to make. So we chose a low-angle static shot that gave us an establisher and conveyed that our characters were secretly tailing the agent. It ended up saving us time on the shoot day and working nicely in the edit.

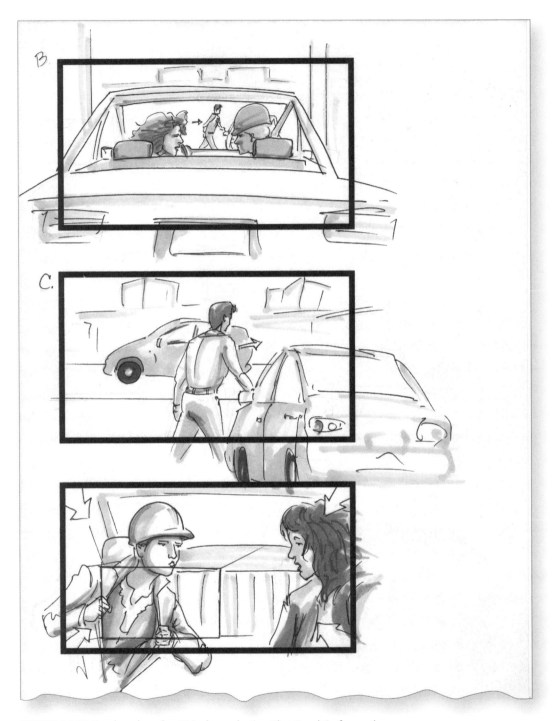

FIGURE 4.2-12. Storyboard number 11 in the production. Shot B and C of scene three.

FIGURE 4.2-12A. Rachel and Michele talking about the next step.

FIGURE 4.2-12B. The Man walking into the bar.

FIGURE 4.2-12C. Rachel showing off her dress.

Compare the storyboard page (Figure 4.2-12) to frames from the short film (Figures 4.2-12a – 4.2-12c).

Commentary

The Director

In the last shot of this page, Rachel reveals that she is wearing a dress under her overalls. I had the storyboard artist board a snap-zoom to move the focal point from a two shot into a close-up of the exposed dress. But as we watched the performance, we chose not to zoom in and allowed the scene to end on Rachel's victorious smile instead. I felt this small moment added to Rachel and Michele's competitive relationship in the film. This is another example that illustrates how events on set can change what was intended in the boards.

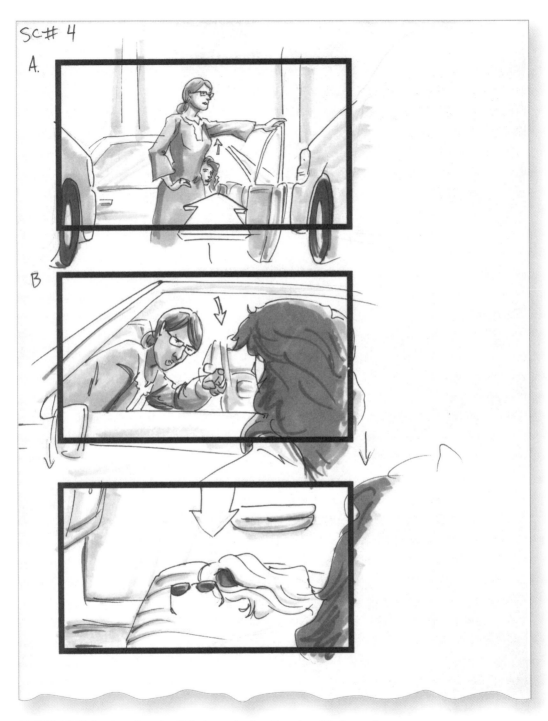

FIGURE 4.2-13. Storyboard number 12 in the production. Shots A and B of scene four.

FIGURE 4.2-13A. This shot was made into slow-motion in editing.

FIGURE 4.2-13B. Rachel telling Michele to stay in the car.

FIGURE 4.2-13C. Michele coming up with an idea.

Compare the storyboard page (Figure 4.2-13) to frames from the short film (Figures 4.2-13a – 4.2-13c).

Commentary

The Director
In the boards, there was one frame indicating a forward camera move toward Rachel as she victoriously exits the car. We filmed the shot as boarded, but we decided to get it both pushing in and pulling out. We also got it in two different frame sizes; medium-wide and medium-close-up. I ended up using the push-in and the push-out camera moves in the edit, making a micro montage.

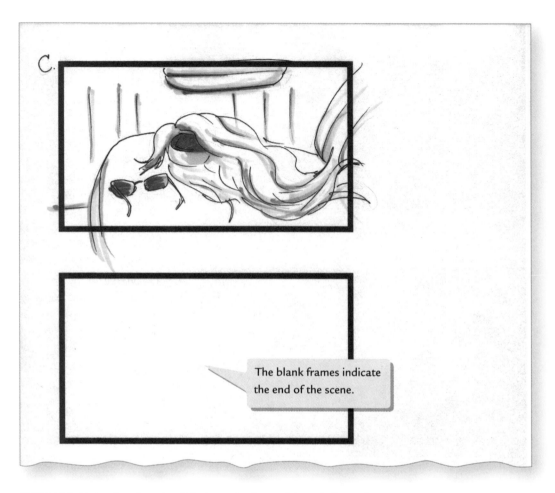

The blank frames indicate the end of the scene.

FIGURE 4.2-14. Storyboard number 13 in the production, and the end of scene four.

This storyboard and shot ended scene four and day one of filming. Because of some bad weather, we had to change the shooting schedule around. Some of what we originally planned to do on day one was moved to day two and vice versa. When things are changed on the fly like that it is important to go over everything with the crew to make sure we are all on the same page. We used the storyboards to go over the changes in what would be done so our cast and crew could adjust. All in all, it was a relatively smooth first day, in spite of the inclement weather.

Compare the storyboard page (Figure 4.2-14) to the frame from the short film (Figure 4.2-14a).

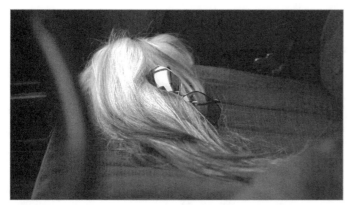

FIGURE 4.2-14A. The wig and sunglasses on the car seat.

Commentary

The Producer
We almost forgot this shot. It was the end of the day and we were almost out of time, so everyone was rushing. But, luckily the shot was drawn in the boards. It was a good reminder.

Our next set of storyboard-to-actual shot comparisons begins with scene 5.

FIGURE 4.2-15. This is a photograph from the first day of shooting. This director has the storyboards in his hands and is crossing off the frames after each shot is filmed.

FIGURE 4.2-16. Storyboard number 14 in the production and the start of scene five.

FIGURE 4.2-16A. Rachel's entrance into the bar.

FIGURE 4.2-16B. Rachel trying to look inconspicuous.

FIGURE 4.2-16C. Michele's slow-motion entrance into the bar.

Compare the storyboard page (Figure 4.2-16) to frames from the short film (Figures 4.2-16a – 4.2-16c).

Commentary

The Producer

For the location of the short film, we had to find a spot that could accommodate all of our different scenes both inside and outside. Ideally we wanted to stay in the same area for the two-day shoot. Morin's Diner worked out perfectly. They had some experience with film crews in the past when Morin's Dinner was featured on the TV show *Good Eats*, so were very accommodating. The storyboards made it easy for me to show them what we were doing and how we were going to use their space. This was helpful to them because they were able to adjust the seating of their customers around our shoot. This worked well, especially in the front bar area, because there were multiple entrances. The storyboard artist used the location photographs in the drawings and even drew the shape of the tables and chairs so it was very clear to everyone where the action and camera were planned to be positioned.

FIGURE 4.2-17. Storyboard number 15 in the production, showing shots D, E and F.

FIGURE 4.2-17A. Rachel and Michele taking up positions.

FIGURE 4.2-17B. Someone new enters the bar.

FIGURE 4.2-17C. Rachel and Michele taking up new positions.

Compare the storyboard page (Figure 4.2-17) to frames from the short film (Figures 4.2-17a – 4.2-17c).

Commentary

The Director
In the shot of everyone at the bar, we looked at the blocking of the action and decided that looking down the length of the bar was the better angle as opposed to looking across it, which was how it was boarded. This allowed us to cover their movements toward the back of the room as well. We covered them with a camera move that ran the length of the bar. This added a sense of urgency to Rachel's walk as she moved to the end of the bar, beating Michele for a closer position to the action.

FIGURE 4.2-18. Storyboard number 16 in the production, showing shots G and H.

FIGURE 4.2-18A. Looking over their shoulders Rachel and Michele are watching The Man.

FIGURE 4.2-18B. The mystery woman and The Man at a table, talking.

FIGURE 4.2-18C. The mystery woman is up to something.

Compare the storyboard page (Figure 4.2-18) to frames from the short film (Figures 4.2-18a – 4.2-18c).

Commentary

The Director

Here, rather than shoot the side angle that was boarded, we set up a wide master shot of the poisoning scene that was over the shoulder of Rachel and Michele. This change did several things: it gave us a better looking shot, it included the agent and the villain—which allowed me to join all four characters in one frame— and we were able to see what was happening in all of the action. The inclusion of all four characters in one frame made the edit more interesting, since the other shots were all tighter frames.

FIGURE 4.2-19. Storyboard number 17 in the production, showing shots I, J, and K.

FIGURE 4.2-19A. The mystery woman slipping something into The Man's drink.

FIGURE 4.2-19B. Rachel's reaction close-up shot.

FIGURE 4.2-19C. Michele's reaction close-up shot.

Compare the storyboard page (Figure 4.2-19) to frames from the short film (Figures 4.2-19a –- 4.2-19c).

Commentary

The Director

For the close-ups of Rachel and Michele, we stayed with the over-the-shoulder angle and captured their performances in profile. These frames continued to keep the agent and villain in the background. I felt that this framing increased the tension of the scene since the audience can now see the action of the poisoning happening in the background while our two heroines are frantic in the foreground.

FIGURE 4.2-20. Storyboard number 18 in the production, showing shots L, M, and N.

FIGURE 4.2-20A. Michele flings food as a distraction to stop The Man from drinking from the glass.

FIGURE 4.2-20B. The food flung into The Man's drink.

FIGURE 4.2-20C. The mystery woman reaches behind her for more poison.

Compare the storyboard page (Figure 4.2-20) to frames from the short film (Figures 4.2-20a – 4.2-20c).

Commentary

The Director
In the script, a plate of chicken wings was brought out to the couple. During the shoot, we eliminated the chicken wings and left it with just fresh drinks being brought over. Even though we shot close-ups of the poison being poured into the fresh drinks, I chose to stay with the two shot in the edit because it played better.

FIGURE 4.2-21. Storyboard number 19 in the production, showing shots O, P, and Q.

FIGURE 4.2-21A. The mystery woman keeping The Man distracted.

FIGURE 4.2-21B. She pours a liquid into the second drink.

FIGURE 4.2-21C. The Man is unaware of what is going on.

Compare the storyboard page (Figure 4.2-21) to frames from the short film (Figures 4.2-21a – 4.2-21c).

Commentary

The Sound Recordist

With storyboards, I can think, ahead of shooting, on areas I can place the mikes to capture the best sound. The boards give me a sense of the style the director is going for. This can change how I capture the audio. I have a better understanding of what kind of ambient sounds or wild sounds the director might be looking for.

FIGURE 4.2-22. Storyboard number 20 in the production, showing shots R, S, and T.

FIGURE 4.2-22A. Rachel has to think fast.

Compare the storyboard page (Figure 4.2-22) to frames from the short film (Figures 4.2-22a – 4.2-22c).

Commentary

The Director

We were only able to afford two replacement shirts for our agent for the part where Rachel squirts him with ketchup. This gave a total of three takes to get the squirting shot right. So, for each angle of this scene, we shot the action right up to the point of the squirting and cut. Then we moved to the medium shot, depicted here, to execute the actual squirting of the ketchup. We were able to get it in only two takes.

FIGURE 4.2-22B. Rachel's turn to make a distraction.

The Producer

We tested how far the ketchup would squirt out of the bottle before the shoot. We knew we only had a few takes and had to find out how far back we should hold the ketchup.

FIGURE 4.2-22C. The Man with ketchup all over his face.

FIGURE 4.2-23. Storyboard number 21 in the production and the end of scene five.

FIGURE 4.2-23A. Illidia is finally identified.

FIGURE 4.2-23B. The showdown starts.

Compare the storyboard page (Figure 4.2-23) to frames from the short film (Figures 4.2-23a – 4.2-23b).

Commentary

The Director
The close-ups of Michele and Illidia, the villain, as they confront each other, were added as a suggestion of the director of photography. He did not feel that we had the confrontation in a dramatic enough way in the two shot. He suggested getting them in close-ups to punch up the drama. It worked out quite nicely.

FIGURE 4.2-24. Storyboard number 22 in the production and the start of scene six.

FIGURE 4.2-24A. Michele looking for Illidia.

Compare the storyboard page (Figure 4.2-24) to frames from the short film (Figures 4.2-24a – 4.2-24c).

Commentary

The Director
The fight sequence was originally scripted to be outside, but the weather prevented us from doing that. We were fortunate enough to be shooting in a location that had multiple dining areas that were not in current use, so we used a brick room with an open center that worked for us, visually and practically, in terms of space for the stunts.

FIGURE 4.2-24B. Illidia is gone.

FIGURE 4.2-24C. Illidia sneaks up on Michele.

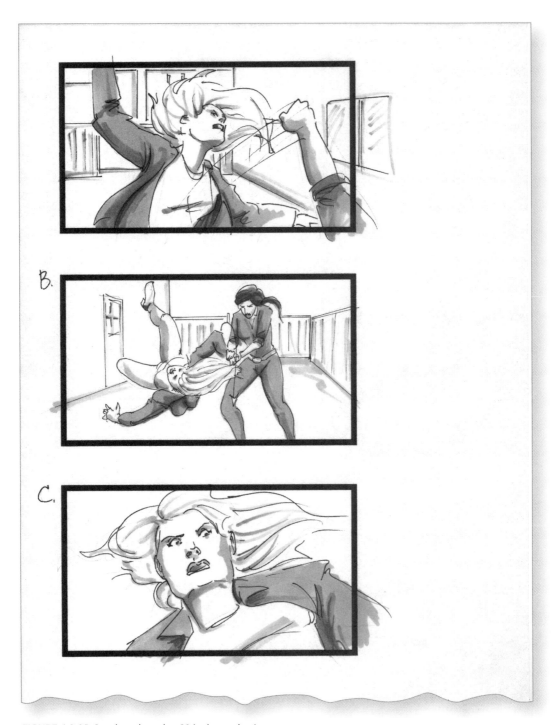

FIGURE 4.2-25. Storyboard number 23 in the production.

FIGURE 4.2-25A. Illidia pushes Michele in a hand-held shot.

FIGURE 4.2-25B. She knocks down Michele.

FIGURE 4.2-25C. Michele is on the ground.

Compare the storyboard page (Figure 4.2-25) to frames from the short film (Figures 4.2-25a – 4.2-25c).

Commentary

Cast Member

"When you are on a set that has storyboards, they can guide you to know what to expect with your shot list, and that is huge, because then you can concentrate on what you need to do rather than being confused. Even if it is just stick figures, it is helpful.

I like how they tell me the depth of field, because I can see if it is a three or two shot and if the frame is tight, plus how much I am in focus. For an actor it is good to know. The director is doing so much already on set and is busy talking with other members of the crew; it is nice to be able to see all these things without having to ask the director.

FIGURE 4.2-26. Storyboard number 24 in the production, showing shots D and E.

FIGURE 4.2-26A. A canted shot of Illidia.

FIGURE 4.2-26B. Someone grabs Illidia from behind.

FIGURE 4.2-26C. Rachel is no match for Illidia.

Compare the storyboard page (Figure 4.2-26) to frames from the short film (Figures 4.2-26a – 4.2-26c).

Commentary

The Director
The fight scene was a great deal of fun to shoot! My plan of boarding the key elements of the scene and finding the rest by letting the camera act as a viewing bystander worked. We got some nice angles, and we were able to get the chaotic feel of the *Bourne* films that I wanted.

FIGURE 4.2-27. Storyboard number 25 in the production, showing shots F, G and H.

FIGURE 4.2-27A. Rachel's reaction shot.

FIGURE 4.2-27B. Illidia knocking down Michele again.

FIGURE 4.2-27C. The Man shows up.

Compare the storyboard page (Figure 4.2-27) to frames from the short film (Figures 4.2-27a – 4.2-27c).

Commentary

The Gaffer

The boards allow all departments to understand what shot they are trying to create. In that regard, it helps them understand where the camera will be, where the lights should be placed, and even what wardrobe will be needed. When I review the boards, I have a better idea of what is going to happen with the shot, which allows me to prepare the equipment before the director comes over to discuss it.

I have worked on sets without storyboards and it is just confusing. The boards give us more information about scenes and shots, which means we can better prepare. The more prepared we are, the more efficiently we can work.

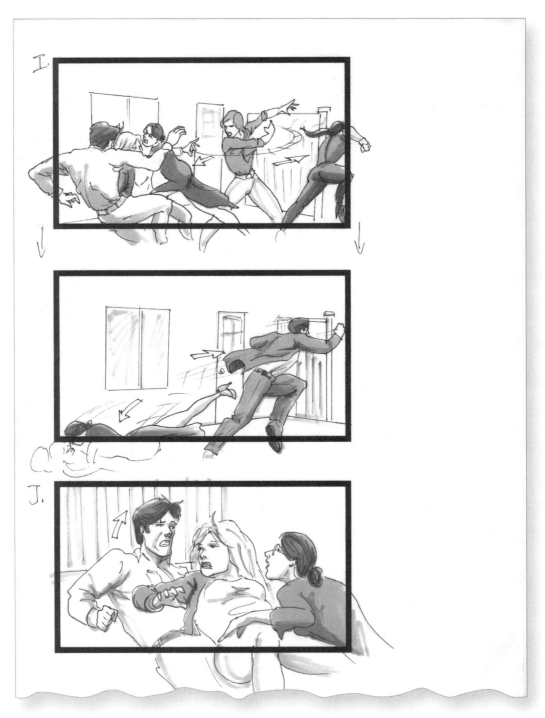

FIGURE 4.2-28. Storyboard number 26 in the production, showing shots I and J.

FIGURE 4.2-28A. Illidia pushes Rachel and Michele into The Man.

FIGURE 4.2-28B. Illidia making her escape.

FIGURE 4.2-28C. A three shot showing everyone on the ground.

Compare the storyboard page (Figure 4.2-28) to frames from the short film (Figures 4.2-28a – 4.2-28c).

Commentary

The Producer

Time was starting to become a factor, especially since we had to change things and move inside due to bad weather. However, a strong plan B and a flexible location really helped. For the most part, we were able to follow the original storyboards with only slight modifications, which helped the crew make up some time.

FIGURE 4.2-29. Storyboard number 27 in the production, showing shots K, L, and M.

FIGURE 4.2-29A. The Man thanks both Rachel and Michele for looking out for him.

FIGURE 4.2-29B. A two shot of Rachel and Michele.

FIGURE 4.2-29C. Rachel and Michele, pleased with their work.

Compare the storyboard page (Figure 4.2-29) to frames from the short film (Figures 4.2-29a – 4.2-29c).

Commentary

The Director

This film was shot rather unusually in that the scenes were filmed in script order. They are usually shot out of order because, typically, location restraints, cast availability, and many other factors prevent shooting in script order from happening. After two days of shooting, with stunts and all, we ended principle photography with the final interchange between Rachel and Michele. We shot the fight scene at the end of the last day, and we were running out of time. I was not able to get the close-ups we had boarded for the final dialogue. I chose, instead, to cover Rachel and Michele in a wide and a tight two shot. Even though I would have rather had the close-ups for the edit, allowing the two shot to play out helped to slow things down to allow the audience to catch up with the story.

FIGURE 4.2-30. The last storyboard for the film *Overtime*.

FIGURE 4.2-30A. The last shot for the film. It is a wrap.

Compare the storyboard page (Figure 4.2-30) to frame from the short film (Figure 4.2-30a).

Commentary

The Producer
This is the final shot of the film. I am happy to say, even with our changes and weather issues, we stayed on schedule for most of the shoot.

After viewing these sequences of storyboard frames and film stills, you can understand that the storyboards are a valuable tool on location and during production.

BRIEF REVIEW OF TERMS:

ACTION An event or series of events that form part of a dramatic plot; also it is the word that is yelled as a cue that the filming of a new take is about to start.

PRODUCER The individual who creates the conditions for making movies. The producer initiates, coordinates, supervises, and controls matters such as fundraising, hiring key personnel, and arranging for distributors.

STUNTS Acrobatic or dangerous actions.

TAKE A single, continuous filmed performance without interruption of the run of the camera.

WILD TRACK Sound recorded without images.

WRAP "It's a wrap!" is a phrase used by the director to signal the end of filming.

4.3 - Updated boards because of on-site changes

The following are two examples of changes that needed to be made on the short film, *Overtime*. Although these are both changes that happened on the fly, we included a modified storyboard to demonstrate what it might look like if the changes had been caught ahead of time.

In every production, there is conflict and change that happens both in pre-production and on set. Budget constraints, weather issues, and equipment failure are just a few examples of what can hinder your schedule. When unexpected changes occur they can cause a great amount of confusion, especially when they affect the way a scene will be filmed. Updated storyboards can really help to communicate the new plan. In this case, the new boards do not need to be refined. Even a quick sketch distributed to the crew will serve as a good guideline.

Scene #1

For your reference, this frame is marked as "A" on our shot list and is part of the opening sequence of the movie. Below is a description of the original idea, which was a single shot ending on Michele in the car.

Commentary

The Director

In this scene, we were forced to change our location and the position of our picture car at the last minute, for safety reasons. The original street had far too much traffic on it for us to work without a police detail. The traffic noise would have also been an issue for sound recording. The change added length to what was already an extensive shot. Unfortunately, we were not able to capture the shot well enough so that each part worked. With each take there was always a portion of the shot that got botched due to a timing or mechanical error.

To remedy the issue and properly capture all of the action, we covered the screen-time of the original boarded shot with multiple angles that would correct the shortcomings of our master. When changes occur, it is best to re-board your shot or scene to reflect the revision. Although we did not have the time or luxury to make the board changes on set, the examples illustrated in Figures 4.3a, 4.3b, and 4.3c show what would have been done if we had caught the issue early, during location scouting.

FIGURE 4.3A. This is the original storyboard sketched.

Original storyboard

FIGURE 4.3B. An updated storyboard frame.

Updated storyboard

FIGURE 4.3C. This is a still photograph from the actual shot sequence.

Actual shot

Many times, change happens on the fly, and re-boarding is often not an option. There are other times when it is necessary, however. One common example of this might be during a location scout. This is when the key members of the crew meet at the film location. They use the boards to go over each shot and evaluate whether it is possible or not. Often changes need to be made. This would be a great time to re-board the scene because filming has not yet begun. Another example is when something unexpected happens on set. The change may be too elaborate to effect without re-boarding, and it is pushed to the following day in order to allow time for proper preparation.

Scene #5 - INT BAR- DAY

This frame is noted as "F" in both the shot list and storyboards. It was reworked for editorial reasons to enhance the storytelling of the film.

Commentary

The Director

This camera angle was chosen over the boarded shot because it was more visually stimulating and it worked better for capturing the blocking of the actors. Changes like this are common on the set, because once confronted with the reality of how a scene actually works, with live people moving and contributing to the scene, often times it takes on its own life. The filmmaker then needs to be able to adapt to what they see if they like it, or rework the scene to better suit their vision.

The Storyboard Artist

When revisions need to be made to the boards, it is important to treat the scene as if you were starting from scratch. This is especially true if the changes are significant. While not every board may need to be redrawn, you want to make sure that the new changes are working within the entirety of the scene. For instance, you may want to ask yourself how the new shot will fit between preceding and upcoming shots.

Figures 4.3d, 4.3e, and 4.3f depict the change of only a single shot, but sometimes an entire scene is rewritten. New action, characters, art direction, or locations could be introduced, and each has to be referenced for accuracy in order to reproduce their likeness. When significant changes like this occur, the chance of mistakenly drawing elements from the discarded scene is possible. Being diligent in gathering and updating the new information will go a long way toward preventing mistakes.

FIGURE 4.3D. This is the original storyboard sketched.

FIGURE 4.3E. An updated storyboard frame.

FIGURE 4.3F. This is a still photograph from the actual shot sequence.

Original storyboard

Updated storyboard

Actual shot

4.4 - The shot list-to-film comparison

Overtime

SHOT LIST

SC#1

> A- MS- City Street, Camera **GLIDES** tilted toward the ground revealing high heels in full stride. We tilt up to reveal Rachel wearing overalls and carry a utility bag. We swing OTS and continue to track with her capturing her rhythmic step. She trips. (MASTER)–Rachel settles at the corner and ruffles through her utility bag. She looks up at window checks her watch then spots a familiar car pulling up. Rachel turns away then walks to the car, talks to Michele and jumps in as the Man exits building. Car follows Man.

> A1 MCU- Rachel's Face as she walks.

> B- MS (OTS)- Rachel pops down into driver's side window, scares Michele.

> C- MS (OTS)- Michele.

> D- FS- Man (from inside car)

SC#2

> A- 2SHOT *(dutch)*- Rachel and Michele scrunched in car.

> B- CU Mirror (HH)- CAM pushing in.

> C- 2SHOT (Pass window)- Rachel and Michele untangle themselves, pop up & drive off.

SC#3

> A- WS *(low angle)*- EXT BAR, CAM **GLIDES** off a parked car as the Man's car pulls into lot. Michele's car pulls in and lingers behind.

> A1-2 SHOT- Rachel and Michele in car.

> B- 2SHOT (behind car)- Rachel and Michele watch the Man enter the bar.

> C- INSERT – Man entering Bar.

> D- MCU – **SNAP ZOOM** as Rachel reveals clothes.

FIGURE 4.4-1. The first page of the shot list, including scenes one through three.

As previously stated, the shot list is often used in conjunction with the storyboards. Because that was the case for *Overtime*, we have included the shot list in this section to compare to the final cut of the film. For the most part, the filmed image matches the shot list except for a few areas that were changed during production.

Compare the shot list (Figure 4.4-1) to frames from the short film (Figures 4.4-2 – 4.1-14).

FIGURE 4.4-2. Shot SC#1 - A

FIGURE 4.4-3. Shot SC#1 - A1   *FIGURE 4.4-4.* Shot SC#1 - B   *FIGURE 4.4-5.* Shot SC#1 - C

FIGURE 4.4-6. Shot SC#1 - D   *FIGURE 4.4-7.* Shot SC#2 - A   *FIGURE 4.4-8.* Shot SC#2 - B

FIGURE 4.4-9. Shot SC#2 - C   *FIGURE 4.4-10.* Shot SC#3 - A   *FIGURE 4.4-11.* Shot SC#3 - A1

FIGURE 4.4-12. Shot SC#3 - B   *FIGURE 4.4-13.* Shot SC#3 - C   *FIGURE 4.4-14.* Shot SC#3 - D

SC#4 – EXT BAR – MOMENTS LATER

A- FS (*slo mo*)- CAM, low angle, **SLIDES** in as Rachel exits car.

B- MS (OTS)- Rachel drops into pass window. Tilt down to reveal wig and glasses.

C- CU- Wig and glasses.

SC#5 – INT BAR- DAY

A- WS (MASTER)- Rachel walks up to bar as the Man orders a drink at bar. Michele enters and walks to the bar. Rachel moves closer and bumps man. Woman enters everyone sits.

B- CU- beer slams on bar counter.

C- MS (*slo mo*)- Michele enters bar.

Deleted Shot

D- 3 SHOT- Rachel notices Michele enter. Michele takes position next to Man. Cover to when Michele sits at table.

E- MS- CAM **SLIDES** as Ilidia enters bar and meets with Man. He leads her to table.

F- WS- Man moves to table with Ilidia.

G- 2 SHOT- Man and Ilidia sit.

H- CU- Ilidia at table. Tilt to reveal her powdering wings.

I- CU- Ilidia puts powder in Man's drink.

J- CU – Rachel

K- CU- Michele

L- CU- Man at table

M- WS- They stand. Ilidia knocks Michele over and exits.

FIGURE 4.4-15. The second page of the shot list, including scenes four and five.

Compare the shot list (Figure 4.4-15) to frames from the short film (Figures 4.4-16 – 4.4-31).

FIGURE 4.4-16. Shot SC#4 - A

FIGURE 4.4-17. Shot SC#4 - B

FIGURE 4.4-18. Shot SC#4 - C

FIGURE 4.4-19. Shot SC#5 - A

FIGURE 4.4-20. Shot SC#5 - B

FIGURE 4.4-21. Shot SC#5 - C

FIGURE 4.4-22. Shot SC#5 - D

FIGURE 4.4-23. Shot SC#5 - E

FIGURE 4.4-24. Shot SC#5 - F

FIGURE 4.4-25. Shot SC#5 - G

FIGURE 4.4-26. Shot SC#5 - H - With reveal

FIGURE 4.4-27. Shot SC#5 - I

FIGURE 4.4-28. Shot SC#5 - J

FIGURE 4.4-29. Shot SC#5 - K

FIGURE 4.4-30. Shot SC#5 - L

FIGURE 4.4-31. Shot SC#5 - M

SC#6 – EXT BAR – CONTINUOUS

A- FS (MASTER)- CAM *GLIDES* in as Michele storms out of the bar. Swing around to behind Michele to reveal Ilidia gone. Ilidia steps into frame and fight ensues with Rachel entering. The Man comes and Illidia escapes. Rachel and Michele are victorious.

B- WS- Fight - Illidia throws Rachel and Michele at Man and escapes. Man says thanks.

C- CU- Michele on ground.

D- CU- Illidia- Tilt up to Illidia's hand as she's about to strike. Rachel grabs Illidia.

E- MCU- Fight, float between Rachel & Michele

F- FS- Man

G- 3SHOT- Rachel, Man and Michele. Cover through end of scene.

H- CU- Michele

I- CU- Rachel

FIGURE 4.4-32. The last page of the shot list, including scene six—the final scene.

Compare the shot list (Figure 4.4-32) to frames from the short film (Figures 4.4-33 – 4.4-41).

Sometimes the boards and shot list are kept separate, as they were in our project; on other occasions they are married into one document, with the boards on one side and the shot description on the other. How the boards and shot list are formatted will most likely be at the discretion of the director. Because the boards were used separately from the shot list for *Overtime,* space was reserved on the right side of each storyboard page to allow for notes to be included, as seen in Section 4.2. This is a common way to format a page of empty board frames because annotations, whether they be written or typed, are often added to clarify or augment the image.

FIGURE 4.4-33. Shot SC#6 - A

FIGURE 4.4-34. Shot SC#6 - B

FIGURE 4.4-35. Shot SC#6 - C

FIGURE 4.4-36. Shot SC#6 - D

FIGURE 4.4-37. Shot SC#6 - E

FIGURE 4.4-38. Shot SC#6 - F

FIGURE 4.4-39. Shot SC#6 - G

FIGURE 4.4-40. Shot SC#6 - H

FIGURE 4.4-41. Shot SC#6 - I

Commentary

The Director

Sometimes, when I create shot lists, they end up being descriptive, while other times they are brief and written in short hand. As I started working on the shot list for *Overtime,* it was lengthy since I had long camera moves and specific ideas for blocking. I chose to leave the shot list and boards separate, since I had a good deal of description. I later went back and trimmed the shot list to what is presented in this book. A few of the shot descriptions are lengthy, but most are brief and common for what could be encountered in the job field.

4.5 - Cast and crew credits for *Overtime*

The following is a list of cast, crew, equipment, and location for the short-film production of *Overtime*.

The *Overtime* cast and crew

Cast
Rachel
Ramona Taj

Michele Estavanti
Leighsa Burgin

FBI Agent
Fiore Leo

llidia Snow
Alisha Finneran

Street Guy
Ron Thibideau

Police
Jonathan Torta

Crew
Director
Vladimir Minuty

Original music score
David Frederick

Director of Photography
Mike Pecci

Writer
Eric Mulder

Producer
Stephanie Torta and Vladimir Minuty

1st Assistant Camera
Tony Fernandez

Gaffer
Dave Provenzano

Sound Recordist
John Gage

Sound Design and Mix
Grey Moore

Storyboard Artist
Vladimir Minuty

Production
Jonathan Torta

Production
Ron Thibideau

The *Overtime* equipment and location

Grip Electric Equipment
Provided by Talamas

Location
Morin's Diner

Cameras
Canon 7D

SUMMARY

This chapter provided a detailed account of a working project—the short film *Overtime*. The sections that compared storyboards with the corresponding film stills included commentaries from various cast and crew members. This chapter gave a first-hand account of an actual film production as it was worked. Comparisons were made that bridged the difference between what had been conceived in preproduction opposed to what actually was shot on site. To demonstrate this, we included comparisons of drawn boards with on-site changes, and shot lists with the actual shots. All of this information can also be found on the DVD included with this book.

ON DVD

REVIEW QUESTIONS: CHAPTER 4

1. What are the views of the cast, producer, director, sound recordist, storyboard artist, and director of photography concerning the use of storyboards?

2. What are the reasons storyboards are sometimes changed?

3. How are storyboards used during production?

4. How do storyboards complement a shot list?

1. Discuss or write about your personal experience, or a movie you have watched, using what you have learned about camera angles, placement, and movement.

2. Discuss problems that might occur in preproduction and production and how they change a storyboard.

3. Discuss why the original storyboard can be different from the final storyboard.

4. Discuss the different views of the director, photographer, producer, storyboard artist, and director of photography.

APPLYING WHAT YOU HAVE LEARNED

1. Use a script of your own or one from this book and develop a storyboard depicting one scene.

2. Use a script of your own or one from this book and develop storyboards depicting all of the scenes.

3. Use a script of your own or one from this book and develop a shot list.

4. Film a short movie using a shot list and storyboards that you created.

5. Form a small group and work on a movie project. Then work on the same project and change roles.

6. Pick a group of still film-frames from the chapter and identify the types of camera shots.

PART **3**

BEYOND THE PAGE

FIGURE PO3. A storyboard frame shaded with use of computer tools.

CHAPTER 5

Technology and Storyboards

Technology and Storyboards

OVERVIEW AND LEARNING OBJECTIVES

In this chapter:

- 5.1 – Conceptualizing for visual effects (VFX)
- 5.2 – Storyboard use in animatics
- 5.3 – Digital creation with graphic tablets and touch screens
- 5.4 – Computer software for storyboard rendering

5.1 – Conceptualizing for visual effects (VFX).

In Chapter 1, we discussed how and when storyboards are used as a communication tool and as a plan for production and postproduction. In this section, we will focus on visual effects (VFX) and animatics and why, with the advances in technology, the importance of storyboards has never been greater.

Visual effects (VFX)

One of the many uses of storyboards is to help the conceptual understanding of a scene. Scenes that involve *special effects (SFX)*, *visual effects (VFX)*, stunts, and complex camera setups are just some of the types of scenes that might be difficult for the crew to visualize. Because visual effects are different types of imagery that are created and integrated into the footage in postproduction, they can be hard to visualize during preproduction and production. With reduction in production costs and the development of powerful computers, the use of *computer-generated imagery (CGI)* is becoming more popular in moviemaking. .

In Figure 5.1-1, we have a storyboard frame showing a scene of a UFO attacking. In the past, one method to film the UFO was to build a physical

FIGURE 5.1-1. A storyboard frame shows a UFO that is not a physical model but is a computer-generated image that will be placed into the scene during postproduction.

model and to shoot the model live with the action of the actors. Although traditional ways of creating different effects are still used, the majority of effects today use CGI. Regardless of the final postproduction process, the role and importance of the storyboard does not change.

> **BRIEF REVIEW OF TERMS:**
>
> **CHROMA KEY COMPOSITING** An editing technique that combines two images or frames; one color of one image or frame is made transparent, revealing the other image or frame behind it.
>
> **COMPUTER-GENERATED IMAGERY (CGI)** Art created with the use of a computer; it can be static or dynamic.
>
> **GREEN SCREEN** Often used in chroma key compositing because green is the least amount of color in skin.
>
> **SPECIAL EFFECTS (SFX)** Practical effects that alter reality, created on set. Normally part of the live-action shoot.
>
> **VISUAL EFFECTS (VFX)** Different types of imagery created and integrated into the footage in postproduction.

Storyboards featuring visual effects are used not only as a communication tool for the cast and crew, but also as a plan for postproduction. Because the filming of the live action is shot before the creation of the visual effects, these scenes need more detailed preproduction planning, in preparation for postproduction, than is necessary for other scenes.

For example, during a shoot, the cast stands in front of a large *green screen* that, using computer-generated imagery (CGI) and *chroma key compositing*, will later be turned into a vast space ship with alien technology. The full scope of the scene could be lost without the help of storyboards to depict the background and the action of the scene for the cast and crew to look at before shooting.

> *The use of storyboards for visual effects is similar to the manner in which animators use storyboards as an outline plan for their full animation drawings.*

NOTE

It is important that all the footage needed to successfully integrate the CGI in postproduction is captured during the shoot in production phase. It is much easier to take the time to plan each shot, storyboard each scene, and make sure all the footage needed is filmed than it is to realize a live action shot is missing or does not cover all the aspects needed when in postproduction. Inadequate planning or oversights cause problems, making it necessary to schedule re-shoots, gathering all the actors and crew back, and inflating budget costs.

Be as detailed as possible during preproduction in developing the shot list and storyboard for scenes involving visual effects. This will save valuable time and money later in the project.

Figures 5.1-2 through 5.1-5 show an example of visual effects being used in a scene that is divided into parts, and the storyboard for the shot. During the live filming of the scene, the cast and crew would be shooting the action in front of a green screen (Figure 5.1-2). Separately, a development team would generate the UFO and background imagery digitally (Figures 5.1-3 and 5.1-4).

In postproduction, the live-action footage is combined with the CGI ship and background for the completed scene. Figure 5.1-5 is an example of a storyboard frame for this scene; it shows both the live action and CGI. Compare

FIGURE 5.1-2. A drawing of an actor standing in front of a green screen for a scene that will be enhanced with computer-generated imaging (CGI) in postproduction. Because during the shot the cast and crew might see only a green screen, they rely on the storyboards for a reference to how the shot will look after postproduction.

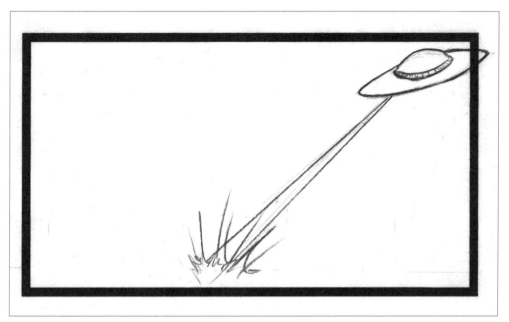

FIGURE 5.1-3. This frame is a drawing of the UFO that will be computer generated and later used as part of the movie scene.

FIGURE 5.1-4. A drawing of a background that represents what will be created with computer-generated imagery for the scene.

FIGURE 5.1-5. A storyboard drawing representing the live action and computer-generated image of a scene. In the live action, the cast and crew will be shooting a frame like that shown in Figure 5.1-2, with the actor in front of the green screen.

the action, look, and feel of Figure 5.1-2 to Figure 5.1-5. It is impossible to interpret the scene correctly by looking at only one part of the scene. The storyboard frame shows how the scene will look after completion in postproduction and helps the cast and crew conceptualize the action, look, and feel of a scene.

5.2 – Storyboard use in animatics

Storyboards are also sometimes used as building blocks to help create an animatic for the film or gaming project. An animatic of the short-film project, *Overtime,* is on the accompanying DVD as an example.

Animatics

As we learned in Chapter 1, an animatic combines images of a storyboard, still photographs, or computer-generated 3D images edited in a sequence and synchronized with a soundtrack. In the past, storyboards were filmed in sequence with zooms and pans to simulate the motion of the scenes. An audio track or music track is then edited to the footage to create the animatic.

With the advancements in technology, computer editing or sideshow software enables quick and easy animatic development.

Animatics give the filmmakers a better idea of how the flow of motion, timing, and sound all work together. Any potential problems can be resolved before the production phase of the project.

Figure 5.2 shows a series of stills with the accompanying dialogue from the script. With movie editing software, the storyboards were assembled to play in a sequence with pans and zooms. The audio and music tracks were edited with the running of the sequence.

A variety of computer software programs can be used to create an animatic. It is best to find one that fits your project's needs and your budget. Some software is user-friendly and is common in the workplace; others are more specialized for movie production and the learning curve to become proficient will be steeper. Some of the many software programs available include:

- **Adobe® Premiere®**
  by Adobe Systems Incorporated
  www.adobe.com/products/premiere/

- **Camtasia Studio®**
  TechSmith Corporation
  www.techsmith.com/camtasia/

  This program was used in making the animatic of *Overtime*, which you will find on the DVD

- **Final Cut Pro®**
  by Apple® Inc.
  www.apple.com/finalcutstudio/finalcutpro/

- **Microsoft® PowerPoint 2010®**
  by Microsoft Office
  office.microsoft.com/en-us/powerpoint/

- **Nero Vision XtraTM**
  by Nero Ltd.|
  www.nero.com/eng/vision-xtra-overview.html

FIGURE 5.2. Stills and dialogue from an animatic.

5.3 - Digital creation with graphic tablets and touch screens

In Chapters 3 and 4, we followed the film project, *Overtime,* using common traditional methods in creating storyboards. Pencil and paper is still the most-often used form in drawing storyboards, however, new technology is gaining in popularity. In this section, we will discuss graphic tablets and touch screens in greater depth.

Graphic tablets

A graphic tablet is a computer tablet that allows a user to hand-draw graphics into a computer, in a manner similar to using a pencil and paper. Ironically, the better the graphic tablet is, the more closely to pencil and paper it performs. Storyboard artists do use graphic tablets for drawing boards, although the tablets are tied to workstations. This makes it difficult to use graphic tablets during meetings and on location. Pencil and paper are still primarily used on these occasions.

Storyboards artists draw not only from scratch, using graphic tablets; they also scan their drawings into the computer for touch-ups, using the features provided by the tablets and the accompanying software. For example, in Figure 5.3-1, the artist used the smudge and blur tools to change the appearance of the camera focus. The pressure sensitivity of the tablet allows artists to use the digital tools as if they were using conventional smudge tools such as blending stumps or kneaded erasers.

Advancements in technology continue to provide more features for the graphic tablets. These include a wider selection of types of paper and drawing pens. For a storyboard artist, these advancements are appreciated, however, until the graphic tablets become more portable, their use for drawing storyboards will be limited. Figures 5.3-3 and 5.3-4 are "before" and "after" storyboard images that were shaded with the use of a Wacom® Intuo4TM graphic tablet.

Some features to look for in a graphic tablet are:

Pressure sensitivity
Pressure sensitivity is one of the most important features when using a graphic tablet. It allows users to control the tablet pen as they would a normal pen. The sensitivity controls line thickness, pressure applied, angle of

FIGURE 5.3-1. A storyboard that was enhanced by using smudge and blur tool effects with a graphic tablet to show a change in camera focus.

the pen, transparency, and color. The higher the pressure sensitivity, the more closely to pencil and paper the graphic tablet performs.

Software interface

Depending on your computer's capabilities, there are different types of computer software. Some packages are bundled with the graphic tablet. Other packages can be purchased separately. For an effective workflow, find one that fits your needs and skill level. Figure 5.3-2 is a screenshot of the interface for Corel® Painter™ Sketch Pad software.

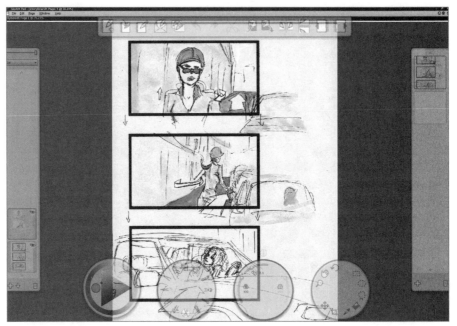

FIGURE 5.3-2. A screenshot of a storyboard work in progress using a Wacom Intuos4 graphic tablet with Corel Painter Sketch Pad software.

Size

Common sizes for graphic tables are 4x5, 6x8, and 9x12. Some manufacturers are making tablets to more closely resemble a wide-screen format. The size of the tablet is not an indicator of a more powerful tablet, but an increase of surface space on which to draw. Choosing an overall size should be according to personal preference and desk space.

Pen

The graphic tablet pen and the button placement on the pen should feel comfortable when drawing. On some tablets, there are additional accessories and types of pens that can be used. Some pens have an erasing end. Depending on the tablet, the pens can be free moving or tethered. In addition, most tablets can be set up for right- or left-handed use.

Cost
Tablets can be expensive at the professional level; however, prices are starting to decrease for the home market. Wacom is a major manufacturer of a variety of graphic tablets, priced according to the various features offered.

Some of the types of graphic tablets are:

- **Aiptek Slim Tablet™**
  by Aiptek
  www.aiptek.com/Tablets/ST12/Features/

- **Monoprice®**
  www.monoprice.com/products/subdepartment.asp?c_id=108&cp_id=10841

- **Wacom® Bamboo™**
  by Wacom
  www.wacom.com/bamboo/

- **Wacom Cintiq®**
  by Wacom
  www.wacom.com/cintiq/

- **Wacom Intuos4®**
  by Wacom
  www.wacom.com/intuos/

Some of the types of software used:

- **Adobe® Photoshop®**
  by Adobe Systems Incorporated
  www.adobe.com/products/photoshop/family/

- **Corel® Painter™ Sketch Pad**
  by Corel Corporation
  www.corel.com/servlet/Satellite/us/en/Product/1231253537915#tabview=tab1

Some of the pros and cons of graphic tablets are:

Pros

- An artist is able to draw directly into the computer.

- The pressure sensitivity allows the artist to draw as if using a pencil and paper.

- Once scanned in or drawn, a storyboard can be easily adjusted.

FIGURE 5.3-3. A storyboard frame before shading using a graphic tablet.

FIGURE 5.3-4. A storyboard frame after shading by using a graphic tablet.

Cons

- Time is a factor, with quick changes needed in meeting and on set.

- Graphic tablets are not very portable.

Touch screens

One of the most notable technological advances is in touch screen technology for portable devices and workstations. One of the drawbacks of graphic tablets is that they are not as mobile as pencil and paper. Touch screen technology has become mainstream with the advances made to portable devices.

Although many devices are portable, the lack of pressure sensitivity is a major drawback for storyboard artists. Until pressure sensitivity becomes a feature of these devices, most storyboard artists will not find them as effective as pencil and paper.

With vast changes in this field occurring continually, it is recommended that you perform a key word search in a Web browser for the latest information. We have, however, provided a list of some of the devices that feature touch screen technology:

- **Android® tablets**
  by a variety of manufacturers

- **iPad®**
  by Apple Inc.
  www.apple.com/ipad/

- **NoteSlate®**
  by NoteSlate®
  www.noteslate.com/

- **Surface®**
  by Microsoft®
  www.microsoft.com/surface/

Some of the pros and cons for touch screens are:

Pros

- Some devices are portable.

- Your workstation travels with you.

Cons

- Portable touch screens lack pressure sensitivity.

- Time involved in using software to draw rather than pencil and paper.

- Need a computing device.

- Learning curve with new software can be steep.

5.4 – Computer software for storyboard rendering

In Chapter 1, we briefly touched upon some different types of storyboard software. There are many different kinds, ranging from complex to simple, free to expensive.

Computer Software

Pencil and paper is still the more common way to create storyboards, because stick figures are effective and quickly drawn, and time is normally a factor in moviemaking. Computer software packages, however, can be both a 2D and 3D rendering tool.

If you have the time, various computer software programs are good tools for rendering scenes in 3D and, once created, are easy for making changes to the camera point of view, focus, and perspective. Once a scene is made, a user can manipulate the cameras, lighting, background, angles, pre-made props, and sequence of movements with just a few mouse clicks. This helps to conceptualize the scenes and shots in preproduction.

Computer programs help the storyboard artist in a variety of ways, from simple touch-ups on boards drawn on paper, to enhancements, to full 3D rendering of the scene. Time is a crucial factor in dealing with full rendering with the computer, for a storyboard artist. Many times, the boards are used more as a communication device for the director to cast and crew; to work out ideas on shots and as a guide during the production phase, the boards do not need to be fully rendered. Storyboards are worked and re-worked in meetings and on set. This makes it difficult to spend the time needed to design a 3D scene on a workstation.

If time is not a factor, however, computer packages enable directors and other filmmakers the ability to design their scenes to gain a clearer understanding of how the story will be told and whether the shots will work together as they envisioned. Non-artists can use built-in features (such as pre-made 3D models) to create scenes beyond the stick figures. Figure 5.4 shows examples of pre-made 3D models and different camera views.

Some features to look for in a storyboard program are:

- 3D models
- Animation
- Built-in animatics
- Caption placement
- Drag and drop interface
- Drawing tools
- Easy-to-navigate interface
- File import and export
- Import text and scripts
- Lighting options
- Layering
- Multiple cameras
- Object-drawing styles
- Pan and zoom
- Playback of the film
- Printing your storyboards
- Sound capabilities
- Template library
- Timeline features
- Transitions between frames

FIGURE 5.4. Here are screenshots taken from a storyboard that was drawn using computer softwear.

Some of the pros and cons of storyboard computer software are:

Pros

- 3D model capabilities
- Easy to move in 3D space
- Camera and lighting placement
- Easy-to-add audio and music tracks
- Faster to animate

Cons

- Time involved in using software to draw rather than pencil and paper
- Reliance on computing device
- Learning curve with new software could be steep
- Lack of portability for meetings and on set

Although it is recommended that a key word internet search be performed for the most recent reviews and updates, we have provided a partial list of storyboard computer software programs:

- **FrameForge Previz Studio 3™**
  by Innoventive Software, LLC
  www.frameforge3d.com/Products/FrameForge-Previz-Studio-3/

- **SketchUp® Pro**
  by Google™
  sketchup.google.com/

- **Springboard™**
  by Six Mile Creek Systems
  6sys.com/

- **StoryBoard Artist Studio**
  by PowerProduction Software™
  www.powerproduction.com/artist_studio.html

- **StoryBoard Pro**
  by Atomic Learning™
  www.atomiclearning.com/storyboardpro

- **Storyboard Pro**
  by Toon Boom™
  www.toonboom.com/products/storyboardpro/

SUMMARY

Pencil and paper is still the common way to create storyboards. Stick figures are effective and quickly drawn in storyboarding, and time is normally a factor in moviemaking. With the advances in technology, however, the various computing devices are becoming increasingly similar to pencil and paper. It is only a matter of time before the computing devices are portable, have pressure sensitivity, and are sufficiently powerful to run complex storyboard software packages with ease.

REVIEW QUESTIONS: CHAPTER 5

1. What are the advantages and disadvantages of drawing paper storyboards?

2. What are the advantages and disadvantages of using digital storyboards?

3. What two groups are special effects traditionally divided into?

1. Why have the advances in technology increased the importance of storyboards?

2. As technology advances, what could be the next step in using storyboards?

3. Would the use of paper for drawing storyboards decline in the future because of digital storyboards?

4. How are storyboard used in animatics?

APPLYING WHAT YOU HAVE LEARNED

1. Explain the following abbreviations and why they are important to storyboarding: VFX, SFX, and CGI.

2. Explain the terms: green screen, graphic tablet, touch tablet, animatics.

3. Create a PowerPoint (or use another computer software package) presentation with frames from your storyboard.

4. Try different computer software packages for storyboard and animatic creation.

GLOSSARY

Many of the words in this list have multiple meanings or uses. This glossary lists their definitions as they apply to the filming and gaming industries.

1.33:1—an aspect ratio; includes television and computer screens; also called 4:3 or Academy Standard

1.66:1—an aspect ratio that is 16mm film or European Projection

1.78:1—an aspect ratio; high definition; the video widescreen standard used in high-definition television; also called 16:9

1.85:1—an aspect ratio that is the American and United Kingdom widescreen standard for theatrical film and 35mm ratio

2.39:1—an aspect ratio for 70mm, Cinerama®, CinemaScope, and other super-widescreen formats

1.43:1—an aspect ratio for IMAX; 70mm-wide film that runs through the camera and projector sideways; allows for a physically larger area for each image

16MM—sixteen millimeter refers to the width of the film with an aspect ratio of 1.33:1 standard and TV, 1.66:1 super

35MM—thirty-five millimeter filming gives a frame aspect ratio of 1.85: 1

ACTION—event or series of events that form part of a dramatic plot; also, a word that is yelled before a new filming take is about to start, as a cue to perform

ACADEMY APERTURE—in 35mm film, the full frame exposed by the camera, with an aspect ratio of 1.33

ACTOR / ACTRESS—a person who acts in a play, film, broadcast, and other forms of media

ADDED SCENES—shots or script changes that are added after preproduction

AERIAL SHOT—an extreme high-angle shot that is usually done with a crane; it also can be done with airplanes and helicopters

ANGLE SHOT / ANGLE—the directional relation between the camera and the object at which it is pointed

ANIMATIC—combined images of a storyboard or still photographs edited in a sequence and synchronized with a soundtrack

ANIMATION—the techniques used to simulate motion through creating frames individually and then editing them as one sequence

ART DEPARTMENT—members of the crew who are responsible for all visual and artistic elements of a project

ART DIRECTOR—the person who determines the staging requirements for a production and often designs the sets or supervises their building and dressing

ASPECT RATIO—the relationship of the height of the frame to its width

ASSOCIATE PRODUCER—the person who is under the direct supervision of the producer; sometimes a junior associate

ATMOSPHERE—the surrounding or pervading mood, environment, or influence

BACKDROP—the background of an event; setting that is created to represent an environment

BACKGROUND ARTIST—the person in charge of creating the art that will appear in the rear of a set

BEAT—the momentary time unit imagined by an actor in timing actions

BLOCK / BLOCKING—to plan or rehearse in order to work out the movement of the camera and placement of the cast and crew for a shot or scene

BLOCKBUSTER—a project that has, or is expected to have, wide popular appeal or financial success

BLUESCREEN—actors and objects are placed in front of a large blue (or green) background to later be superimposed onto another image

BODY DOUBLE—a person whose body is shown in substitution for a leading actor

BOOM—a pole carrying an overhead microphone above the scene

BOOM OPERATOR—the person who controls the overhead microphone on the boom and assists in placing microphones

BOOM SHOT—also called a jib or crane shot, and refers to a high-angle shot, sometimes with the camera moving

BOX RENTAL—payment to crew members for use of their own equipment for a project

BUDGET—the total amount of money allocated for a specific purpose during a specified period of time

CALL SHEET—a list of cast and crew members and the schedule of when they are needed for different scenes

CAMERA—a device that records still or moving images

CAMERA ANGLE—the point of view from which the camera photographs a subject or scene

CAMERA CREW—a team in charge of the operation of a camera

CAMERA MOVEMENT—a change in subject view, frame, or perspective of a shot, made by the movement of the camera

CANTED FRAME—also known as a Dutch angle; a shot that is tilted 25 to 45 degrees to one side, causing horizontal lines be at an angle

CAMERA ROLL—each individual recording of the camera

CAST—actors in a play, film, broadcast, and other forms of media, collectively

CAR MOUNT—shots taken with the camera mounted on an automobile or other type of vehicle

CHANGE PAGES—script changes during production

CHROMA KEY COMPOSITING—an editing technique for combining two images or frames, making one color of one image or frame transparent to reveal the other image or frame behind it

CINEMATOGRAPHER—the person controlling a filming camera, especially one who is in charge of shooting and artistically capturing images; sometimes known as a director of photography

CINEMATOGRAPHY—the artistic creation of moving images using light and cameras

CLOSE-UP (CU)—a framed shot taken at close range wherein the subject is larger than the frame; often from the top of the head to the top of the chest of a person

CO-PRODUCER—the person who co-supervises and controls the finances, creation, and public presentation of a project

COMIC BOOK—narrative works of art in separate panels often accompanied by dialogue

COMPUTER-GENERATED IMAGERY (CGI)—art created with the use of a computer; can be static or dynamic

COMMERCIAL BOARDS—normally color on large sheets of paper and very detailed; at times, designed by advertising agencies for their clients

CONCEPT BOARDS—very detailed illustrations focusing on the location, set, background scenery, or a dramatic event

CONTINUITY—the seamless physical detail from one shot to another within a scene

COVERAGE—shooting a scene from many different angles in order to properly tell the story

CRANE SHOT—a shot taken by a camera on a crane and often used to capture a view of the scene from above or to move up and away from the start point; see also boom shot

CREDIT—the recognition or approval for an act, ability, or quality

CREW—the group of people working together in the production but not appearing in the production

CUT—the call "Cut" stops filming when in production; in editing, to make an abrupt change of image or sound, or changing from one shot to another

CUTAWAY—a shot of part of a scene, filmed from a different angle and/or focal length from the master shot, of action not covered in the master shot

CUTSCENE—in video games, the stopping of game play for the player to watch in-game action and mini-movies mostly uncontrolled by the player

DAILIES—the dailies are the first, unedited print of movie film, usually viewed after a day's shooting; can also be called "rushes"

DAY OUT OF DAYS—a chart used by filmmakers to tally the number of paid days for each cast member

DEPTH OF FIELD—the level of clarity behind and in front of the plane on which the camera is focused

DIRECTOR—the person who controls the creative aspects (translating the script into images and sounds) of a project and instructs the cast and crew

DIRECTORS GUILD OF AMERICA (DGA)—a labor union for the motion picture industry

DIRECTOR OF PHOTOGRAPHY (DP)—a movie photographer who is in charge of shooting the movie and is responsible for achieving artistic and technical decisions related to the images

DISSOLVE—a transition between scenes; one scene fades away and the other fades in simultaneously

DOLLY / DOLLY SHOT—a moveable platform that enables a movie or video camera to move during shots

DRAFTSMAN—a person skilled in technical drawing for purposes such as set building

DUTCH TILT, DUTCH ANGLE—also known as a canted frame; a shot that is tilted 25 to 45 degrees to one side, causing horizontal lines be at an angle

EDIT—the act of deleting, arranging, and placing together shots and sounds in order to construct a flowing sequence

EDITORIAL BOARDS—storyboards that tell a story and are sometimes taken from scripts

ESTABLISHING SHOT—a wide shot (WS) or a long shot (LS) that gives an audience a basic orientation to the geography of a scene

EXECUTIVE PRODUCER—the person who brings the financing together for a project and generally handles business issues; might also be a financier of a film

EXTERIOR (EXT)—a representation in visual art of the outdoors or scene shot outside a studio

EXTRA—a performer hired to play a minor, nonspeaking role

EXTREME CLOSE-UP (ECU / XCU)—reserved for dramatic impact; the shot may show just the eyes of an individual

EXTREME LONG SHOT—a view from an even greater distance than a long shot (LS); often people-size objects are small within the frame

FADE—the gradual diminution or increase in the brightness or visibility of an image in cinema or television

FADE IN—to appear or be heard gradually

FADE OUT—to disappear gradually

FIRST UNIT—the team that shoots all scenes involving the major actors of the film

FLASHBACK—a literary or cinematic device in which an earlier event is inserted into the normal chronological order of a narrative

FLASHFORWARD—an interjected scene that takes the narrative forward in time from the current point of the story

FOLLOW SHOT—the camera follows the action of a subject from a fixed position

FOREGROUND—the part of a scene or picture that is nearest to and in front of the viewer

FORMAT—the specific type of media used to capture an image, i.e., 1.85:1 35mm film, 1.78:1 HD; also, the type of equipment used to photograph and project and screen the media

FRAME—the viewing area as seen by the camera lens

FREEZE FRAME—a still, motionless scene or image in the course of a shot made by running a series of identical frames or by stopping at one desired frame

FULL SHOT (FIGURE)—sometimes called a long shot (LS), a frame captures the relative distance between the top of a person's head to their feet

GAFFER—the lead electrician responsible for the lights

GAME ENGINE—the software designed for the creation and development of computer games

GAMEPLAY—the interaction the player has with the computer game

GAMEPLAY BOARDS—the map of actions and paths the player of a computer game has available throughout the course of a game

GRAPHIC NOVEL—narrative works of art that tell a story using art; often accompanied by dialogue

GRAPHIC TABLETS—a computer tablet that allows a user to hand-draw (like using a pencil and paper) graphics into a computer

GREEN LIGHT—permission to proceed with a project

GREEN SCREEN—often used in chroma key compositing because green is the least amount of color in skin; also, see BLUE SCREEN

HAND-HELD—a shooting technique; the camera is held in the operator's hands

HIGH ANGLE—the camera shot usually set above the eye line of the subject

HIGH DEFINITION (HD)—video having higher resolution than standard definition (SD) and digitally broadcast using video compression

HOT SET—an action actively being filmed or about to be filmed in a take

IMAX— a 70mm-wide film that runs through the camera and projector sideways, allowing for a physically larger area for each image

INDEPENDENT FILM / INDIE—a film produced outside of the Hollywood studio system

INSERT—a shot of action already covered in the master shot but from a different angle or focal length

INTERIOR (INT)—a picture or rendering of the inside of a building or room

JUMP CUT—an edit that removes the middle section of a continuous shot and joins together the beginning and end of the shot; any moving objects in the shot will appear to jump to a new position

KEY FRAME—a drawing that defines the starting and ending points of any smooth transition

LAP-DISSOLVES—also called dissolves; two scenes momentarily overlap during a transition from one to the other

LETTERBOX—the practice of transferring film shot in a widescreen aspect ratio to standard-width video formats while preserving the film's original aspect ratio

LIGHTING—the use of artificial and natural sources, for aesthetic or practical reasons, while illuminating a scene

LINE PRODUCER—the person who manages the budget of a motion picture; also may manage the day-to-day physical aspects of the film production

LOCATION / FILMING LOCATION—the place where some or all of a project is produced, in addition to or instead of using constructed sets

LOCATION DIAGRAMS—Overhead diagrams used to illustrate camera placement within a set or location for particular shots

LOCATION SOUND—any sound recorded at the shoot

LONG SHOT (LS)—sometimes called a full shot (FS); taken where the frame captures a broad view of the environment and away from the subject

LOW ANGLE—a camera shot usually below the eye line of the subject

MAJORS—motion pictures normally with a large budget, sizeable in scope

MARTINI SHOT—the final shot of the day

MASTER SHOT—the filming of an entire scene, from start to finish, and from an angle that generally keeps all the players in view

MATCH CUT / MATCH DISSOLVE—a cut from one scene to a completely different scene with the objects in the two scenes occupying the same place in the frame

MATTE ARTIST—the artist who combines two or more image elements into a single, final image

MATTE SHOT—a small portion of the shot is a live action shot, the rest is masked to show a different background or foreground image

MEDIUM CLOSE-UP (MCU)—a medium close-up shot cropped between the shoulders and the chest

MEDIUM SHOT (MS)—a shot from a medium distance and normally from the waist up

MONTAGE—short shots edited into a sequence to condense narrative; often used to suggest the passage of time

MOTION CAPTURE—the process of capturing movement and translating the information into a digital form or model

OBJECTIVE SHOT—a shot not seen from the viewer's point of view

OFF SCREEN (OS)—the action or sound that takes place out of the frame of the camera

OVER-THE-SHOULDER SHOT (OTS)—the shot of someone or something taken over the shoulder of another person; the back of the shoulder and head of this person is used to frame the image of whatever (or whomever) the camera is pointing toward

PAN—to move a camera to follow an object or create a panoramic effect

POINT-OF-VIEW SHOT (POV)—a shot that shows what a subject is looking at, through the camera perspective

POSTPRODUCTION —the general term for all stages of production occurring after the actual shooting, ending with the completed work

PREPRODUCTION—the process of preparing all the elements involved in a project before actual shooting

PRINCIPAL PHOTOGRAPHY— the primary phase of production during which the project is actually shot, as distinct from preproduction, postproduction, or reshoots

PRODUCER—the person(s) who creates the conditions for making movies; they initiate, coordinate, supervise, and control matters such as fundraising, hiring key personnel, and arranging for distributors

PRODUCTION—the process of actual shooting all the elements for a film project

PRODUCTION ASSISTANT (PA)— the person responsible for various aspects of a production; tasks can vary greatly depending on budget and specific requirements of a production

PRODUCTION BOARDS— sometimes taken from scripts to tell a story, they reflect the director's or developing team's ideas on the story and camera shots

PRODUCTION COMPANY—the group of people responsible for the development and physical production of a project

PRODUCTION DATE—the date shooting will start

PRODUCTION DESIGNER—the person responsible for the overall design of the project; the key creative role, working directly with the director and producer to create settings and develop the style to visually tell the story

PRODUCTION ILLUSTRATOR—the person responsible for drawing elements of the production and sometimes storyboards

PRODUCTION MANAGER—the person responsible for practical matters in creating the vision of the director or choreographer within constraints of technical possibility

PRODUCTION SCHEDULE—a plan of how the production budget will be spent over a given time scale

PROFILE—a side view of an object or structure, especially of the human head

PROP—an object used in a performance

REACTION SHOT—an actor or actors shown reacting to another actor's action or words, or to an event that is witnessed

REVERSE SHOT (REVERSE ANGLE)—the view of the action from the opposite side of the previous shot

SCREEN ACTORS GUILD (SAG)—a union that represents actors

SCALE—a proportion used in determining the dimensional relationship of a representation to that which it represents

SCENE—the presentation in which the setting is fixed and the time is continuous

SCREENPLAY—a script for a movie, including descriptions of scenes and some camera directions

SCRIPT—a written text of a film

SCRIPT BREAKDOWN—a list of the basics elements of the project, including special items, equipment, and effects that are necessary for the script

SECOND UNIT—a team that shoots footage which is of lesser importance for the final motion picture; typically scenery, close-ups of objects, and other inserts or cutaways

SET—the location where shooting is taking place, either indoors or outdoors

SET DESIGN / SCENIC DESIGN—also known as production design, the creation of scenery and backgrounds

SETUP—each new camera angle, especially when lighting must be moved

SHOOTING SCHEDULE—a plan of each day's shooting for a production

SHOOTING SCRIPT—a version of a screenplay used during the production, using scene numbers and following a well-defined set of procedures specifying how script revisions should be implemented and circulated

SHORT FILM—a film under 60 minutes in length

SHOT LIST—a document listing all intended shots in a film

SINGLE—a shot with the frame encompassing a view of one person or subject

SLUG LINE / SLUG—the text before each scene in a script that details the time and location of the action

SMASH ZOOM—the dolly zoom effect done very quickly

SPECIAL EFFECTS (SFX)—practical effects created on set that alter reality; normally part of the live action shoot

SPEED—the team, camera person, or sound recorder that will call out to acknowledge that they are rolling

STATIC SHOT—the camera and frame do not move when shooting

STEADICAM SHOT—a shot using a mechanism or mount for steadying a hand-held camera

STOCK FOOTAGE—a film or video footage that is not custom shot for use in a specific film or television program

STORYBOARD—a series of drawings, illustrations, or photographs that convey a story or series of events and sometimes includes dialogue

STRAIGHT ON (FRONTAL)—a non-angled view of the subject in the frame

STUNTS—acrobatic or dangerous actions

SUBJECTIVE SHOT—a shot taken from a subject's point of view

SUPER 35—a ratio which includes 70mm, widescreen, Cinerama, CinemaScope, and other super-widescreen formats

SWISH PAN—a panning shot in which the scene moves too quickly to be observed

TALENT—another name for an actor or a cast member

TAKE—a single, continuous filmed performance without interrupting the run of the camera

TOUCH SCREEN—a digital display that can detect and track the location of a touch on the screen

TILT / TILTING—a cinematographic technique in which the camera rotates up or down

TRACKING SHOT—a shot taken while the camera is being moved by means of wheels, as on a dolly

TRAVELING SHOT—a shot taken when a camera moves with the subject

TWO SHOT—a frame encompassing a view of two people or subjects; many common two shots have one subject in the foreground and the other in the background

UNIT PRODUCTION MANAGER (UPM)—an executive who is responsible for the administration of a film; generally responsible for watching all costs on the project, with the intention of delivering the film on budget at the end of principal photography

VISUAL EFFECTS— audio or visual effects that alter reality and are edited postproduction after the live action shoot

VOICE OVER (VO)—narration heard over a scene; also, narration heard at a higher level than a source of music or background sound

WARDROBE DESIGNER—the person responsible for the design of costumes for both film and stage production

WEB SITE NAVIGATION BOARDS—drawings or thumbnails that create connections and map out the navigation of a Web site

WHIP PAN—a type of pan shot in which the camera moves sideways so quickly that the picture blurs into indistinct streaks; commonly used as a transition between shots, can indicate the passage of time and/or a frenetic pace of action

WIDE SHOT (WS)—a shot taken from a distance; reveals where a scene is taking place

WIDESCREEN—70mm, widescreen, Cinerama, CinemaScope, and other super-widescreen formats

WILD TRACK—sound recorded without images

WIPE—a gradual spatial transition from one image to another; one image is replaced by another with a distinct edge that forms a shape

WRAP—a phrase used by the director to signal the end of filming

ZOLLY—a shot involving a dolly and zoom combination

ZOOM—A gradual change in the focal length of the lens; creates the effect of dollying in or out without moving the camera

APPENDIX B

MISCELLANEOUS

- DVD information
- Blank storyboard frames
- Storyboard practice frames
- Extra scripts
- Additional Exercises
- Cast and crew biographies
- References
- Credits

DVD information

The DVD that is included in this book contains a number of additional files and features. Additional scripts, blank storyboard frames, and exercises are included for further study of how storyboards fit into the filming process.

The short film, *Overtime*, is shown in its entirety and in completed form. The book showcased the steps taken in both preproduction and production to make the final film. The DVD also includes the in-real-time film and storyboard comparisons. Using the book together with the DVD allows you to watch the static script become a motion picture.

- Full running of the film, *Overtime*
- Full running of the film, *Overtime*, synchronized with the side-by-side running of the storyboards
- Full running of the film, *Overtime*, synchronized with the visual of the script text and the running of the storyboards
- Full *Overtime* animatic
- A storyboard slide show running in order
- *Overtime* storyboard movie with voice over
- Extra scripts and blank frames
- Additional exercises

FIGURE A.1. A still screenshot from the film, *Overtime,* located on the DVD. The preproduction and production of the film is showcased in the book.

Blank storyboard frames

On the DVD, there are files containing pre-made blank storyboard frames. Following are blank frames for 2.39:1–widescreen and 1.78:1–high definition:

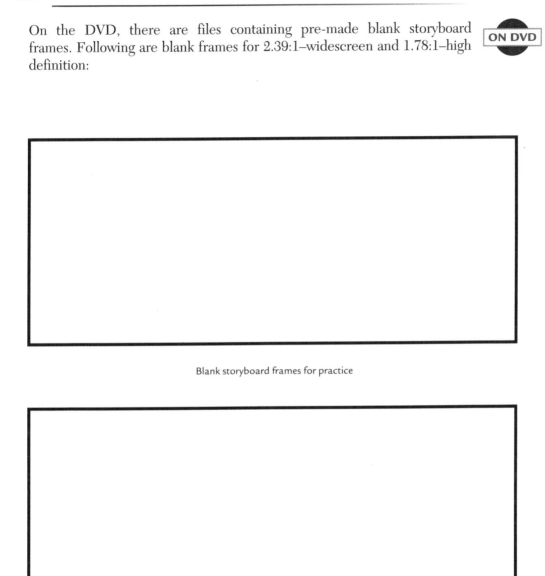

Blank storyboard frames for practice

FIGURE A.2. Storyboard frames (2.39:1–widescreen) for practice drawing.

Blank storyboard frames for practice

FIGURE A.3. Storyboard frames (1.78:1–high definition) for practice drawing.

Storyboard practice frames

Included here are a few storyboard frames to use for creating your own script, shot list, or story, to analyze or to re-draw.

FIGURE A.4. Storyboard frames for practice in creating your own script and shot list.

Extra scripts

On the DVD, there are files containing extra scripts that have not been produced. Below is one of those scripts. You can use these scripts to practice the steps for creating storyboards and for the book exercises.

Playing Ball - The Lion and the Mouse

FADE IN

EXT. BASEBALL FIELD

The Vikings and the Bears are having a scrimmage game in a local baseball field. Nine team members of the Vikings arrive in a huge van with their team's name on the side of the van, expensive uniforms, plus matching sports bags and baseball shoes. Fifteen members of the Bears' team arrive in old cars with their parents; uniforms bought at the local department store and old, mismatched baseball shoes.

The Vikings' coach speaks to his team.

                    VIKINGS' COACH
            Today will be an easy win
            for us. They have only won
            two games this whole season
            and we have won all of our
            games this year. Think
            of today as practice. You
            won't have to play hard
            against them.

The Bears' coach speaks to his team.

BEARS' COACH

Do your best today. We won
our last game and we can do
it again. It doesn't matter
what their record is this
season. This is a new game.
Just do your best!

UMPIRE

Let's play ball!! Batter
Up!

The first Bears' player goes to bat.

VIKINGS' PLAYERS

(chanting) Easy out! Easy
out!

TWO PLAYERS STRIKE OUT

VIKINGS' PLAYERS

(chanting) Easy out! Easy
out!

EXT. OUTFIELD

The third Bears' player hits the ball and the
center and left fielder collide trying to catch
it. The coach goes out to see the injured
players.

VIKINGS' COACH

Both of you have to go sit
on the bench with those
bloody noses. Call the ball
next time!!

EXT. VIKINGS' COACH GOES OVER TO TALK TO THE
BEARS' COACH

              VIKINGS' COACH

              We will have to forfeit the
              game. We do not have any
              players to replace our two
              injured players.

              BEARS' COACH

              Let's finish the game. We
              have extra players. You can
              have two of our players to
              play the outfield.

              VIKINGS' COACH

              Thank you! I appreciate
              that.

EXT. THE GAME CONTINUES

VIKINGS' COACH TALKS TO HIS ASSISTANT COACH

              VIKINGS' COACH

              Our new Bears' players are
              really playing great. They
              are calling the balls and
              are catching them.

              ASSISTANT COACH

              It looks like they gave us
              their best players.

THE BASEBALL GAME ENDS

                    VIKINGS' COACH

          We wouldn't have won the
          game without your players.
          They are very talented. I
          would like to offer them
          the chance to play on our
          summer team.

                    BEARS' COACH

          That would be great! They
          need to increase their
          playing time and they
          could use more coaching
          than I can give them.

VIKINGS' COACH TALKS TO HIS ASSISTANT COACH

                    VIKINGS' COACH

          I was wrong about the
          Bears' team. They don't
          have a good record this
          season and they look
          scrawny, but they helped
          us when we needed it.

          VIKINGS' ASSISTANT COACH

          They could have easily won
          the game when our players
          got injured. We would
          have had to forfeit the
          game but they showed great
          sportsmanship.

FADE OUT

Additional Exercises

1. Discuss or write about a personal experience or a movie you have watched, using storyboarding ideas.

2. Develop a storyboard from one of the scripts included in the book, DVD, or story you have read.

3. Make your own movie and use storyboards.

4. Put a series of photographs or drawings in order and tell a story.

5. Take one picture and tell a story from it and describe what storyboard and shot list you would make.

6. Discuss what you have learned from the book and what surprised you.

7. Summarize each section of the book and discuss the parts that have been most helpful; explain why.

8. Draw the text from the script *Mad Dash*, located on the DVD, into a storyboard page, using the blank frames that are provided.

```
                Excerpt from Mad Dash

Mike turns at the next exit and travels on a
two-lane highway.

                     MIKE
                We got the first green
                light.


                   JENNIFER
                Let's hope our luck
                continues.

They go through a few more lights. Mike is
getting very upset.
```

Blank storyboard frames for practice

FIGURE A.5. Practice (1.78:1–High definition) storyboard frames for drawing.

Cast and crew biography

Cast

RAMONA TAJ

Ramona is an actress and model in Boston. After years of nonprofit work in the arts, encouraging students to pursue their dreams, Ramona decided to make a change and pursue her own dream of acting. Since her first audition in 2009, she has been cast in multiple independent projects, playing both principal and supporting characters. Ramona approaches each project—whether it is acting, modeling, singing, dancing, or working behind the scenes as a member of the crew—with the same enthusiasm and philosophy: *"If a picture's worth a thousand words, then it had best have something to say." www.ramonataj.com*

LEIGHSA BURGIN

Formally trained in the performing and fine arts as well as being an accomplished producer, director, and choreographer, Leighsa has worked extensively in live performances with a number of theater companies for the past ten years. Her impressive body of work spans a wide range of genres from live events, to theater, to television and film.

She is proud to be a founder of and performer in the internationally touring and award-winning theatrical company for *All the Kings Men.* Her most recent film role, aside from *Overtime,* was playing herself in *Play in the Gray,* a documentary about *All the Kings Men.* Her favorite stage credits include the starring role of Mona in *Come Back to the Five and Dime, Jimmy Dean, Jimmy Dean,* Catherine in Arthur Miller's *A View from a Bridge,* and May in Samuel Beckett's *Footfalls.* Leighsa has no favorite venues for performance, though her favorite kind of work is challenging, tough, and boundary stretching.

FIORE LEO

Fiore is a native Bostonian who has been acting since his late teens. He is very active in the local Indy film scene and is beginning to broaden his "acting horizons." He enjoyed working on *Overtime* and is very flattered to be part of this project.

ALISHA FINNERAN

Alisha attended the University of Maine at Orono, where she studied anthropology. After becoming established as a licensed esthetician, she began classes with the New Hampshire Theatre Project. From there she became involved in local theater. In the beginning of this year, Alisha attended a film class at CP Casting in Boston. She became very interested in the subtleties of film and has pursued her interest since. Alisha resides in Maine with her husband.

Crew

MIKE PECCI

Mike Pecci's ability to touch audiences through his films is a credit to his commitment to understand humanity. His work has an emotional quality that can both frighten and pull in audiences, playing off the darkest chasms of the human condition. Working with some of the most deeply hidden places in a character, Mike has created timeless films that impel you to fall in love or cringe with fear.

Trained in film production at the New York Film Academy in 1999, Mike Pecci has since worked with some of Boston and New York's brightest and boldest talents. His music videos have been featured on *MTV2* and *Fuse,* and his films have excited festival audiences for years.

With eight years of experience on the Boston film scene, Mike has cemented a name for himself not only as a music video director, but as an abstractly edgy filmmaker who is undeniably devoted to the art of storytelling. His characters are the faces of his work—passionate, emotional, vulgar, and distorted stories are the basis for some of Mike's most well-received films.

ERIC MULDER

Eric was summoned to Houghton Mifflin Company during the Great Tolkien Wars. Sadly, he succumbed to his wounds and has since died and gone to Harvard. Now laboring for Harvard University Press, he continues to put words on paper. They aren't usually his own words, but no afterlife is perfect.

JOHN GAGE

Sound mixer John Gage has worked in the New England movie industry for eight years; his projects have included many involving people with disabilities. He plays several instruments in a few rock bands, and is in postproduction on his comedy /sci-fi /music-movie, *Elvis's Dream Attack.*

www.newenglandfilm.com/user/ 37515

DAVID FREDERICK

David Frederick is an Emmy-nominated composer who, with years of award-winning work as a composer, continues to inspire audiences through his music and creativity.

In a career that has earned him an Emmy nomination, critical acclaim, and numerous awards, David has proven himself to be a versatile composer in a wide range of musical styles and contexts. David has earned a reputation as an exceptional collaborator, making him a top choice for producers and directors. No matter the genre, medium, or venue, David displays boundless enthusiasm with the ability to engage and connect with the listener through his talent for crafting evocative and memorable new musical worlds. David combines his broad-based musical experience, training, and a strong knowledge of contemporary sounds to easily adapt to any assignment. His true genius lies in the fact that he instinctively has a deep understanding of what the core and emotion of a production is and consequently produces music that is perfectly suited. David is further noted for his gift of unique composition styles, haunting melodies, and support of a filmmaker's vision. Whatever your personal tastes in music, media, entertainment, or popular culture, chances are good that you've had at least a passing acquaintance with the work of David Frederick.

GREY MOORE

"Grey is an extremely talented composer, sound designer, and musician. He brings multiple talents to all of his endeavors, resulting in outstanding quality and creativity." May 16, 2006. Request a new or revised recommendation from David Frederick

References

Begleiter, Marcie. *From Word to Image–2nd edition : Storyboarding and the Film-making Process,*. Michael Wiese Productions, 2010.

Fraioli, James O.. *Storyboarding: A Crash Course in Professional Storyboarding.* Michael Wiese Productions, 2000.

Glebas, Francis. *Directing the Story: Professional Storytelling and Storyboarding Techniques for Live Action and Animation.* Focal Press, 2009.

Pardew, Les. *Beginning Illustration and Storyboarding for Games.* Premier Press, 2005.

Credits

Overtime short film
Vladimir Minuty
Stephanie Torta

Illustrations
Vladimir Minuty

Photographs
Jonathan Torta
Stephanie Torta

Scripts
Overtime and *Mastermind*
Eric Mulder

Playing Ball - The Lion and the Mouse and *Mad Dash*
Diana Torta

INDEX

1.33:1, 38–39, 281
1.43:1, 39, 42, 281
1.66:1, 39, 281
1.78:1, 14, 38–39, 40, 82, 281, 286, 295–296, 303
1.85:1, 39, 41, 281, 286
2.39:1, 28, 39, 41, 281, 295
2D, 20, 182–183, 276
3D, 20, 24, 79, 268, 276–278
16mm, 39–40, 281
35mm, 39, 281–282, 286
70mm, 39, 281, 286, 290–291

A

Academy Aperture, 282
action, 247, 281
actor, 7, 13, 74, 103, 109, 177, 182, 191, 207, 237, 266, 268, 282, 289, 290
actress, 282
AD. *See also* assistant director
added scenes, 282
advertising agencies, 8, 284
aerial shot, 48, 56, 57, 282
agency, 9, 19
American Projection, 39, 41
anatomy, 14
angle, 60, 282–283, 285–287, 289
angles shots, 56, 282
animated films, 20, 25
animated movies, 20
    animatic, 20
    animation, 20
    animator, 20
    motion capture, 20
animatic, 19–21, , 263–264, 268–269, 277, 280, 282, 294
animation, 9, 20, 265, 282
animators, 20, 265
arrow, 7, 14–15, 17, 46–47, 62, 68, 75, 83, 109, 124, 130, 136, 140, 144, 194
art department, 282
art director, 282
artist, 18, 21, 22–23, 32, 41, 76, 87, 103–104, 109, 166, 270, 275, 277
aspect ratio, 4, 14, 16, 17, 36–43, 39, 41, 43, 281, 282, 287
assistant director, 9
associate producer, 282
atmosphere, 282

B

backdrop, 282
background artist, 282
beat, 282
block, 209, 282
blockbuster, 282
blocking, 209, 282
bluescreen, 282
blur, 66, 270, 291
board, 4, 7–9, 41, 60, 70, 72, 76–78, 108, 118, 132, 158, 182, 213, 248, 250, 256
boarded, 13, 19, 20, 23, 126, 130, 166, 193, 197, 211, 215, 221, 223, 245, 248, 250
body double, 282

boom, 7, 62, 283, 282–284
boom shot, 49, 62–63, 284
box rental, 283
brainstorm, 21
budget, 13, 30, 34–36, 78, 87, 107, 195, 248, 266, 269, 283, 287–289, 291

C

call sheet, 283
camera, 48, 98, 283
   angle, 60
   seeing through, 17
   setups, 7, 13, 36, 264
camera angles, 30, 33, 56, 57, 58, 59, 61, 122, 126, 154, 164, 260
camera frame, 14, 16, 38, 39, 48, 66, 68, 72, 79, 119
cameraman, 24, 68, 79
camera movement, 4–11, 14, 17, 32, 36, 45–46, 49, 60–71, 79, 88, 98, 109, 111, 119, 124, 126, 142, 190, 194-195
   boom shot, 49, 62
   car mount, 49, 64
   crane shot, 49, 62
   dolly shot, 49, 60
   follow shot, 49, 70
   hand held, 49
   pan, 49, 66
   smash zoom, 49. 68
   static shot, 49, 64
   steadicam shot, 49, 64
   swish pan, 49, 66
   tilt, 49, 62
   tracking shot, 49, 66
   traveling shot, 49
   whip pan, 66
   zolly, 49, 68
   zoom, 49, 68
camera placement or angles, 44, 48–49, 80, 103, 287
   aerial shot, 48, 56
   canted frame, 48, 60
   high angle, 48, 56
   low angle, 48, 56
   over the shoulder, 48, 56
   profile, 48, 56

   reverse shot, 48, 60
   straight on or frontal, 48, 56
camera shots, 44, 48–75
   field-size or scale, 48
   movement, 49
   placement or angles, 48
canted frame, 48, 60–61, 283, 285
car mount, 49, 64–65, 283
cast, 78–79, 283
cast members, 79, 118, 182
CGI. *See also* computer-generated imagery
change pages, 283
character, 36, 37, 45, 47, 107, 120, 126, 136, 138, 142, 146, 152, 154, 184, 304
character movement, 45, 136, 154
characters, 20, 33, 37, 130, 154, 180, 184, 211, 223, 250, 304, 305
chroma key compositing, 265, 283
cinemascope, 39, 281, 290, 291
cinematic, 17, 22, 285
cinematographer, 35, 38, 283
cinematographic technique, 62, 290
cinematography, 88, 283
close-up, 44, 48–51, 76, 98, 152, 201, 203, 205, 213, 215, 225, 283, 285, 287
comic book, 8, 142, 146, 284
commercial boards, 284
communicate, 4, 10, 25, 30, 31, 47, 76, 80, 86, 87, 118, 174, 248
communication, 8, 9, 11, 13, 31, 33–34, 37, 86, 264–265, 276
computer, 276
   programs, 276
   rendering, 276
   software, 276
computer game, 3, 8, 20–22, 25, 77, 286
   cutscene, 22
   game engine, 22
   gameplay, 22
   gameplay boards, 22
computer-generated, 264–268, 284
computing device, 276, 278
concept board, 8, 284
conceptualization, 10, 33

continuation, 14, 17

continuity, 284

co-producer, 283

coverage, 7, 98, 154, 164, 172, 197, 284

crane shot, 49, 62–63, 283–284

creation, 10, 18, 20–22, 31, 35, 77, 87–88,
184, 263, 265, 270, 280, 283, 286, 289

credit, 284

crew, 77–78, 283–284
    preproduction, 77
    production, 78

crew members, 7, 10, 30–31, 35, 190, 209,
259, 283
    director, 34
    director of photography, 35
    producer, 35
    production designer, 35
    set designer, 35
    storyboard artist, 34

CU. *See also* close-up

cut, 72, 152, 284, 286–287

cutaway, 49, 70–71, 284

cutscene, 20–23, 25, 33, 284

D

dailies, 284

day out of days, 284

depth of field, 284

detail, 4, 8, 19–20, 34–35, 66, 76–77,
80–81, 118, 120, 150, 182, 186, 248, 284

development, 37

development team, 8, 21–23, 33–34, 80,
266

diagrams, 37

director, 6, 9, 11, 17, 19, 30–37, 41, 86–87,
98, 209, 282, 284

director meetings, 37, 106–109

director of photography, 12, 13, 19, 30, 35,
78–79, 106, 190, 203, 207–211, 233, 259,
260, 283–284

Directors Guild of America, 284

director's ideas, 10, 31, 34

director's vision, 7, 10, 35, 37, 44, 87, 106,
118, 174

dissolve, 49, 72–73, 285, 287

dolly, 7, 44, 48-49, 60–61, 64, 66, 68, 120,
285, 290–291

DP. *See also* director of photography

draftsman, 285

draw, 4, 41, 102–103

drawing, 44, 47, 270
    aspect ratio, 41
    frame, 47

drawings, 4, 8–9, 20, 25–26, 29, 34, 37,
76, 80, 86, 102–103, 118, 219, 265, 270,
290–291, 302

drawing the frame, 47

Dutch angle, 60, 283

Dutch tilt, 60, 285

DVD information, 294

E

ECU. *See also* extreme close-up

edit, 72, 285

editing, 20, 23, 44, 48, 49, 72, 74, 77, 80,
152, 154, 197, 203, 205, 215, 265, 269,
282, 283, 284

editorial boards, 285

editorial, editing, and point of view, 49
    cutaway, 49, 70
    establishing shot, 49, 70
    freeze-frame shot, 49, 74
    jump cut, 49, 74
    master shot, 49, 74
    match cut, 49, 72
    objective shot, 49
    point of view shot, 49, 72
    reaction shot, 49
    subjective shot, 49

editorial shot, 70–71, 74

environment, 36, 52, 102, 186, 282, 287

establishing shot, 50, 70–71, 122, 211, 285

European Projection, 39–40, 281

executive producer, 285

EXT. *See also* exterior

exterior, 47, 285

extra, 285

extreme close-up, 48–51, 285

extreme long shot, 52, 285

eye line, 56, 286–287

F

fade, 5, 89, 285, 298, 301
field-size or scale 48, 50, 52
    close-up, 48, 50
    extreme close-up, 48. 50
    extreme long shot, 52
    full or figure shot, 48, 52
    insert, 48, 54
    long shot, 48, 52
    medium shot, 48, 50
    single, 48, 54
    two shot, 48, 54
    wide shot, 48, 52
figure shot, 48, 52
film, 18, 20, 253
filming location, 103, 287
filmmaker, 4, 76, 269, 276, 284
filmmaking, 17, 20, 30, 33, 39, 86, 156
financing, 30, 285
first unit, 285
fixed position, 70, 285
flashback, 285
flashforward, 285
focal length, 54, 68, 70, 284, 286, 291
follow shot, 49, 70–71, 285
foreground, 52, 54, 225, 285, 287, 290
format, 286
frame, 4, 14, 17, 41–45, 50, 283, 286–287
    camera, 14, 48
    drawing, 41
    for film, 17
    height, 43
    inside, 17
    number, 41
    outside, 17
    size, 36
freeze frame, 74, 286
frontal, 290
FS. *See also* full shot
full shot, 52, 286–287

G

gaffer, 79, 241, 258, 286
game
    creator, 4

    developer, 4
    engine, 22, 286
gameplay, 8, 21–23, 33, 80, 284, 286
gameplay board, 8, 22
graphic novel, 8, 76, 286
graphic tablet, 23, 263, 270–275, 280, 286
    cost, 273
    pen, 272
    pressure sensitivity, 270
    size, 272
    software interface, 272
green light, 286
green screen, 265–268, 280, 286

H

hand-held, 49, 75, 286
hardware, 23
HD. *See also* high definition
high-angle, 56, 62, 134, 282–283, 286
high definition, 16, 39, 40, 82, 286, 303
Hollywood, 22, 35, 286
horizontal axis, 58
horizontal line, 60, 283, 285
hot set, 286

I

illustrate, 10, 36, 58, 79, 103, 122, 136, 168, 190, 287
imagery, 37
IMAX, 39, 42, 281, 286
independent film, 35, 286
indie. *See also* independent film
information
    gathering, 37, 85–87
    refining, 110
    used, 37
initialed, 14
insert, 24, 48, 54–55, 286
INT. *See also* interior
interior, 47, 286
internet, 278
interpret, 17, 268
interview, 9, 19, 21

J

jib, 62, 283

jump cut, 49, 74, 286

K

key frames, 41, 79, 287

L

lap-dissolves, 287
lens, 4, 68, 286, 291
letterbox, 287
lighting, 287
line producer, 287
location, 86, 102–103, 182, 287
location diagram, 31, 33, 36, 102–103, 186
location photograph, 36–37, 85, 102–104, 107–108, 120, 182, 219
location scouting, 87
long shot, 48–52, 70, 107, 285–287
low-angle, 48, 56–57, 211, 287
LS. *See also* long shot

M

majors, 35, 287
martini shot, 287
master shot, 48–49, 54, 70, 74, 98, 223, 284, 286–287
match cut, 49, 72–73, 287
match dissolve, 287
matte artist, 287
matte shot, 287
medium close-up, 98, 287
medium shot, 45, 48, 50–51, 109, 231, 287
meeting, 9, 19, 31, 33–35, 79, 85–86, 106, 146, 275
meeting with the director, 31, 37, 87
miscommunication, 77
montage, 288
motion capture, 20, 33, 288
motion pictures, 35
movie photographer. *See also* director of photography
moving platform, 60
MS. *See also* medium shot
music, 258, 268–269, 278, 291, 305

N

narration, 291

non-artist, 23
noninteractive, 22

O

objective shot, 74, 288
object positioning, 7
objects, 4, 15, 17, 31–32, 37, 46–48, 52, 65, 72–74, 105, 186, 282–289
off screen, 47, 288
OS. *See also* off screen
OTS. *See also* over-the-shoulder
outside factors, 13
overhead diagram, 36, 87, 287
overhead illustrations, 36
over-the-shoulder, 46, 48, 58–60, 98, 197, 225, 288
Overtime
    cast, 258, 304
    crew, 258, 304
    DVD information, 294
    script, 88–97
    script with director notation, 111–117
    shoot, 190
    shot list, 98–101

P

pan, 7, 44, 49, 66, 67, 70, 108, 109, 124, 268–269, 277, 288, 290–291
panoramic, 66, 288
pencil and paper, 23, 25, 270–279, 286
perspective, 10–11, 17, 24, 49, 72, 87, 138, 276, 283, 288
photograph, 18, 36, 37, 87, 104, 110, 184
point-of-view shot, 72, 288
portable, 23, 270, 275, 279
portrayal, 7, 25, 32, 76, 150
postproduction, 23, 31, 74, 110, 111, 203, 264, 265, 266, 268, 288, 291, 305
POV. *See also* Point of View shot
preproduction, 7, 31–33, 36–37, 77–78, 85, 87, 104, 106, 111, 119, 288
pressure sensitivity, 270, 272, 274, 275, 276, 279
primary figures, 34
    director, 34

storyboard artist, 34
principal photography, 111, 288
problem, 13, 19, 77, 260, 266, 269
producer, 30, 35, 78, 247, 288
production, 7, 31, 36, 78, 87, 111, 189,
  288–290
production designer, 31, 35, 102, 106
profile, 48, 58–59, 289
prop, 4, 6, 30–37, 76, 85–88, 105–109, 150,
  182–185, 191, 276, 289

Q

quick sketch, 33–34, 76, 102, 118, 191
quote, 13, 24, 33, 77, 79

R

reaction shot, 55, 74, 289
reference, 9–13, 19, 36–38, 44, 87, 104,
  109, 166, 191, 248, 266
rendering, 21, 47, 263, 276, 286
reveal, 52, 142, 213, 291
reverse angle. *See also* reverse shot
reverse shot, 48, 60–61, 289

S

scale, 289
scene, 4, 11, 14, 16, 18, 31, 41, 47, 72, 98,
  152, 266, 289
scenic design, 289
screen actors guild, 289
screenplay, 289
script, 4, 8–9, 11, 30–31, 34, 36–37, 44–47,
  86, 88, 110, 118, 190, 298–289
script breakdown, 88, 289
script notes, 17
script supervisor, 190
SD. *See also* standard definition
second unit, 289
set, 103, 286, 289
  building, 87, 285
  diagrams, 36, 86
setting, 102, 170, 282, 289
setup, 103, 289
SFX. *See also* special effects
shoot, 23, 134, 266

shooting area, 36
shooting schedule, 13, 98, 216, 289
shooting script, 289
short film, 35, 289
shorthand, 45, 181
shot, 14, 47, 98, 207
  common type, 48
  description, 50–75
  example, 50–75
  types of, 49
shot indicator, 17
shot list, 37, 44, 45, 98, 110, 176–181
  film, 252–257
  Reading, 45
  Translating, 44
  Understanding, 44
Shot list, 36, 86–87, 98, 289
shot sequence, 7
single shot, 54, 136, 248, 250, 290
sixteen millimeter. *See also* 16mm
sketch, 21, 30, 33, 44, 76
slug line, 290
smash zoom, 290
software, 20–27, 263, 269–273, 276,
  278–280, 286
sound, 18, 47, 72, 79, 190, 199, 229, 248,
  259, 269, 284, 287–291, 305
special effects, 13, 264, 265, 279, 290
speed, 290
stabilizer, 107, 195
stage, 12, 30, 119, 291, 304
standard definition, 39
static shot, 49, 64–65, 211, 290
steadicam, 49, 64–65, 107, 195, 290
stock footage, 290
storyboard, 4, 19, 290
  anatomy, 14
  animated movie, 20
  artist, 17, 31, 34, 36, 86–87, 106, 184
  change, 248
  comic-book, 8
  commercial board, 8
  comparison, 191–247
  computer game, 20
  concept board, 8

created, 36
creation, 31, 87
detailed, 76
development, 31
digital creation, 270
director, 6
editorial, 8
evolving, 23
frame, 4, 6–7, 11, 13–14, 17, 27–28,
    30, 39, 43–49, 52–56, 66–68, 73–75,
    78, 82-83, 177, 195, 247–251, 261,
    264–268, 274, 293–297, 303
future, 22
gameplay board, 8
graphic novel, 8
hardware, 23
location, 182
page, 4, 14
planning, 37
preproduction, 7, 13, 36
process, 30, 77
production, 36
production board, 8
prop, 184
reference guide, 12
refining, 110
rough, 118–175
script, 6
sequence, 52, 57, 63, 67, 69
shot list, 176
sketch, 33
software, 23
start, 30
talent, 182
technology, 263
type of, 8
types of scene, 13
wardrobe, 184
web site navigation board, 9
what are, 4
what is portrayed, 14
who benefits, 77
why use, 10
storyboards evolving, 23
    hardware, 23
    software, 23
storytelling, 8, 31, 33, 44, 49, 74, 78, 88,

106, 110, 120, 138, 180, 186, 250, 305
straight-on, 58, 205, 290
studio executives, 30
stunt, 13, 235, 245, 247, 264, 290
style, 6, 8, 12, 20, 30–37, 78–79, 87–88,
    105, 106, 111, 156, 177, 184, 186, 229, 288
subject, 14–15, 17, 30, 45–76, 130, 154,
    283–290
subjective shot, 74, 290
super 35, 39, 41, 290
swish pan, 290

T
tablet, 21, 270–274, 280, 286
take, 247, 290
talent, 9, 31, 33, 36–37, 79, 85–86, 102,
    104, 182, 290, 305
technology, 20, 23, 33, 263–265, 269–270,
    275, 279–280
television, 8–9, 38–40, 281, 285, 290, 304
television commercial, 8–9
text, 37
theatrical film, 39, 281
thirty five millimeter. *See also* 35mm
three-shot, 54
thumbnail, 9, 13, 30, 80, 88, 291
tilt, 6, 46, 60, 62, 108–109, 120, 122, 285,
    290
tilting, 62, 108, 122, 193, 290
time line, 87
touch screen, 270, 275, 290
    portable, 275
    pressure sensitivity, 275
tracking shot, 49, 66, 67, 109, 120, 290
traditional, 20, 22, 142, 265, 270
transition, 66, 72, 285, 287, 291
translate, 6, 30, 34, 44–45, 47, 49, 180
traveling shot, 290
two shot, 48, 54–55, 213, 227, 233, 237,
    245, 290

U
unit production manager, 290
updated boards, 189, 248

V

vertical axis, 58
VFX. *See also* visual effect
video camera, 23, 38, 60, 285
video game, 21–22, 33, 80, 284
visual effect, 13–14, 77, 263–266, 291
visualize, 4, 7, 10, 12, 24, 30, 77, 79, 118,
    182, 264
visual reference, 9, 13, 87
visual representation, 30
voice over, 291

W

wardrobe, 30, 36–37, 85, 88, 105, 107, 109,
    150, 184, 186, 241
wardrobe designer, 291
weather, 13, 216, 235, 243, 247–248
web browser, 275
web site navigation board, 9, 291
whip pan, 66, 291
widescreen, 16, 28, 39, 281, 287, 290–291,
    295
wide shot, 44, 47–48, 52–53, 70, 285, 291
wild track, 247, 291
wipe, 124, 291
working relationship, 18
workstation, 23, 270, 275
wrap, 247, 291
written story, 7
WS. *See also* wide shot

Z

zolly, 49, 68–69, 291
zoom, 7, 17, 49, 68–69, 140, 207, 213,
    268–269, 277, 290–291